Praise for *Full Cup, Thirsty Spirit*

"*Book titles are sometimes misleading. Not this one. The book itself is a full cup of life-giving water for thirsty spirits everywhere. Karen Horneffer-Ginter writes wonderfully well about the vexations and vicissitudes of everyday life. A grounded and gifted storyteller with a winsome sense of humor, she teaches a simple spiritual alchemy that can turn daily dross into priceless gold. I love this book so much I read it in one sitting and have already started practicing its alchemy. So read it and use it! You'll be very glad you did.*"

— Parker J. Palmer, author of *Healing the Heart of Democracy, The Courage to Teach,* and *Let Your Life Speak*

"***Full Cup, Thirsty Spirit** is an inspirational and practical guide that helps us track very closely our relationship to joy. Seldom do you find a book that provides comfort, solace, and healing in one place. The total impact is one of simultaneous upliftment and deep nourishment.*"

— Angeles Arrien, author of *Living in Gratitude, The Second Half of Life,* and *The Four-Fold Way*

"*Karen lives fully and passionately in this world. No monk or nun, she lives in the same world that assaults us with relentless demands. Because, like us, she knows this world all too well, we find we can trust her. So when she tenderly offers a gentle insight, points us toward a glimpse of subtle grace, or reveals an unexpected fragrance of wonder in the midst of our familiar parade of daily discouragements, we already belong to her. We see, just as she does, the astonishing surprises that shine their light just barely beneath the surface of our overwhelmed existence. Put away your lists and piles, and allow the beauty of your unopened life quietly to take your breath away. You can do this, Karen reassures us, again, and again."*

— Wayne Muller, author of *A Life of Being, Having, and Doing Enough; Sabbath; How Then, Shall We Live?; Learning to Pray;* and *Legacy of the Heart*

"I wish I'd had **Full Cup, Thirsty Spirit** *with me through the course of my 'serious' grown-up life. In the pause I took to read it, I gained more time and a happier heart."*

— Amy Weintraub, author of *Yoga for Depression* and *Yoga Skills for Therapists*

*"***Full Cup, Thirsty Spirit** *combines advice, story, and practice for those ready to consider changing their pace of life and attaching to an inner self. These are increasingly needed skills in the techno-plugged in world, and Karen shows readers the way to another way. Enjoy—read slowly."*

— Christina Baldwin, author of *The Seven Whispers: Spiritual Practice for Times Like These* and *Storycatcher: Making Sense of Our Lives Through the Power and Practice of Story*

*"***Full Cup, Thirsty Spirit** *is like sharing a table with a dear and wise friend. Karen's stories leave you smiling in recognition and open to her gentle suggestions for more self-awareness. Flavored with Eastern wisdom and Western practicality, this book offers more than one kind of tea. Refreshing and restorative."*

— Karen Maezen Miller, author of *Hand Wash Cold: Care Instructions for an Ordinary Life* and *Momma Zen*

FULL CUP,
thirsty spirit

FULL CUP,
thirsty spirit

Nourishing the Soul
When Life's Just Too Much

Karen Horneffer-Ginter, Ph.D.

INSIGHTS

HAY HOUSE, INC.
Carlsbad, California • New York City
London • Sydney • Johannesburg
Vancouver • Hong Kong • New Delhi

Library of Congress Control Number: 2012948360

Tradepaper ISBN: 978-1-4019-3993-9
Digital ISBN: 978-1-4019-3994-6

15 14 13 12   4 3 2 1
1st edition, December 2012

Printed in the United States of America

*To my beloved Paul, Nathan, and Kenzie
for filling my cup and nourishing my soul in
ways beyond my imagination.*

CONTENTS

TENDING TO OUR THIRST

The rush and pressure of modern life are a form, perhaps the most common form, of its innate violence.

— Thomas Merton

I had never heard the word *yurt* before, but within minutes I realized it was exactly what I'd been looking for. At the time, I was at lunch listening to my friend describe his new project. "I'm building a yurt on some wooded property by a lake."

"A what?" I asked, in a voice muffled by my sandwich.

"A yurt, a Mongolian yurt. It's like a tent or a teepee, but bigger and more deluxe. I'm hoping to build it and move in before winter."

"You're kidding?" I asked, my eyes squinting in disbelief.

"No, no, I'm serious. I got approval from the township, but I was told to describe it as a 'membrane-covered dwelling with a dome at the top.' I guess people freak out a little at the thought of a teepee."

"And you are building this by a lake?" I asked, questioning each word: *you? building? by a lake?* "Like *Walden Pond?*"

"Yeah . . . that's right." He nodded, pleased that I was starting to catch on.

"Oh my God!" I exclaimed. "I want that. I want your yurt!"

I need to pause here, for a moment, to explain a few important things. First, I did understand, even then, that I couldn't really have his yurt. I knew that it was unreasonable to suggest that he should give it to me, and that unlike in the expression *mi casa es su casa,* his yurt is his, and my presence in it would only ruin its fundamental yurt-ness. But all the same, it's a rare moment to have one's needs captured in a tangible form and rarer still to encounter a person who is about to pick up a hammer and bring such a thing into being.

Even that day at lunch, I could see that a yurt wouldn't solve all of my problems, that it would be insufficient to pick up and move to an alternative housing structure. But that didn't stop me.

"Would I have to go before the board to build a yurt in my backyard?" I asked my friend once the dessert had arrived. "Or would it be possible to get some type of invisible fencing?"

"Maybe what you need," he gently offered, "is to create this retreat in your mind. You know, to find some way within to honor your need for balance, or just to accept that as humans we often want things to be other than what they are."

"No, no, I've tried that," I joked. "I'm done with interventions on the inside. I need lumber. I need nails. I'm leaving for Home Depot as soon as we get the check."

The story of my yearning for a yurt and the circumstances surrounding it highlight much of what I see in my therapy practice. So often, I hear clients lamenting: "I've just had so much going on—I haven't had a moment to catch my breath." And it's likely that we'll find ourselves speaking such words—and searching for our own getaway—at one time or another, as we balance the demands of adulthood. Often the more successful we are at carving out a life with meaningful activities and relationships, the more likely we are to get overwhelmed by the demands of all that we've created. It seems this predicament is an inevitable cost that comes from being effective at filling our lives with engagements and commitments. I'm not quite sure why it has to be this way, but I've seen it in my own life as well as in the lives of many people I counsel and teach. The schedules we create with the best of intentions often become too much to bear, and we end up feeling like the sunflowers of late summer, slumped over by the size and heaviness of all that's resting on our shoulders. As Merton's words suggest, we become victims of a self-created violence.

This dynamic can be hard to spot at first, especially if our life's cup is overflowing with good things. It's easier to see and feel the need to slow down and fill up when life is difficult. Either way, however, the qualities of busyness and too much-ness can create an ache in our souls based on their sheer volume. They can keep us from hearing our own wisdom to know what needs to happen in our lives and inside ourselves. They can also leave us feeling disconnected from a sense of gratitude for the things that, deep down, we feel grateful for.

What we need most during these times is to turn our attention within and replenish. We need the very thing that often feels the furthest away. Finding time to slow down can be an obstacle, no question. However, I've come to see that not knowing how and where to begin is often an even greater challenge.

Along with discovering how to create such pit stops for ourselves when we most need them, other shifts are sometimes required if we want to bring our lives into balance and sustain these changes over time. These shifts include reconnecting with what matters most, bringing this awareness into our everyday lives, accessing humor and playfulness when we can, and being present with life's challenges when we must.

This is the book I've wanted to hand to people in response to their predicament of busyness—even though I'm aware that it's not always easy to find time to read. It's the book I've wanted to turn to myself in many moments over the years.

The book's content is organized around six key shifts: honoring our rhythms, turning within, filling up, fully inhabiting our days, remembering lightness, and embracing difficulty. They represent what often gets lost amid life's busyness and what we so often need to reclaim when we're feeling overwhelmed and exhausted. They also reflect the essential ingredients needed to create a vibrant life that we can fully experience and embrace.

We can think of these six shifts in relationship to the cycle of the seasons. Just as we might start the New Year by pausing, taking a breath, and considering the bigger picture of life, the first shift, *honoring our rhythms,* involves taking a look at how we can best support ourselves.

While pausing and slowing down are essential ways of honoring these rhythms, the second shift, *turning within,* represents a more conscious retreat from the doing of life in order to come to know ourselves—and our spiritual connection—more deeply. It mirrors the season of winter, with its shorter days and encouragement to curl up under a blanket and be reflective.

The third shift, *filling up,* focuses on the importance of nourishing ourselves with proper self-care—tending to the garden of our well-being, just as we might literally tend to a garden in the springtime by watering and feeding that which we care about.

The fourth shift, with its summertime feel, is *fully inhabiting our days.* It considers how we can truly show up when we're engaged in life—how we can bring the best of what we've gained from *turning within* and *filling up* right back out into our day-to-day activities and into the service we're offering in the world.

The final two shifts, *remembering lightness* and *embracing difficulty,* provide important tools that balance each other across time. Choosing to make room for both reflects autumn's invitation to take pleasure in joyful harvests and brightly colored leaves, while also recognizing when it's time to let go and be present with life's turns and endings.

The shifts reflect a progression. However, given that there's no one-size-fits-all formula for self-growth, and that life doesn't always unfold in a linear way, you may find that you want to focus on a certain shift that feels especially relevant to your life, regardless of its order.

Instead of viewing these shifts as goals to accomplish and move on from, think of them as tools and reminders that we can return to, again and again, as we move through our days and find ourselves thirsty for balance and renewal.

As you read through the chapters, keep these questions in mind: What shifts most need my attention now? Which ones get forgotten when life is busy? And how might I remind myself, over time, to return to this toolbox?

May the ideas and exercises in each of these sections weave together to enrich your journey, and may they offer the inspiration you need to nourish yourself deeply now and in the future.

HONORING OUR RHYTHMS

She would center her clay, and then keep bringing it out, out, to its edge, and then, pushed to its limit, it would collapse . . . she realized that she was the clay. She had been brought again and again to her edge, only to collapse. The invitation was clear, to live her life close to her center.

— WAYNE MULLER

Like all things in nature, we have an inherent rhythm that moves through us. In some ways, this is obvious. We can sense the pulsing of our heart, and, for most of us, there is regularity to our sleeping and waking. If we live in a place with distinct seasons, we feel shifts in temperature and scenery. We may also notice changes in our wardrobe, our energy level, and the produce available at the market.

Other rhythms move in us as well, although their exact nature differs from one person to another. These rhythms involve our relationship to showing up in the world and taking a break. They involve our capacities for activity, creativity, and engagement, and our need for rest, renewal, and an emptying out of debris.

We live in a culture that often asks us to ignore these deeper rhythms. It dictates that we have little need for rest or time off. I don't know who exactly set up these expectations, but I know they exist because I see their impact on people daily. I hear women and men speaking about how something is being asked of them that they can't deliver and, in turn, feeling like something is wrong with their fundamental nature. These are the people arriving at doctors' offices with complaints of fatigue and aches and a sense of dis-ease that permeates their days. These are the people who feel trapped in the heaviness of life's demands and disconnected from a sense of aliveness.

Matt had worked at a high-powered job for 15 years and established a solid reputation. Being seen as the go-to person gave him a strong sense of satisfaction, but this status also made him feel like he couldn't take time off. "You should see the pile I come back to if I'm gone for even a day. It's just not worth it."

For years, this situation had been acceptable to him, but then he started reconsidering things after needing to go on medication for high blood pressure. "I'm having a hard time relaxing even on the weekends, and it doesn't help that I come home Friday nights and have to turn around and head to church since I agreed to chair an outreach program."

For Todd and Sue, their complaints took a different form. Although neither of them was experiencing health problems, they felt extremely disconnected from each other. As they were working parents of four children, it seemed the only conversations they had were about clarifying who was driving which child where and who was cooking dinner. As Sue commented, "Honestly, it's been so long since we've talked about anything other than day-to-day details, I don't think we even know each other anymore."

For these individuals, their symptoms—physical and emotional—reveal that they are living out of sync with the inherent rhythms of their bodies and lives. Such symptoms provide an inconvenient reality check that tells us that we need more care and attention than we had hoped. It's as though we thought we were labeled with a tag naming us as a hardy plant that can tolerate any conditions, but, in fact, we have a whole set of particular instructions necessary to protect our delicate nature. If we ignore these, it isn't possible to experience vitality or joy in our days.

This reality is neither simple nor easy. We live in a time when few mechanisms for respite exist, aside from serious illnesses and retirement. We live in a place where vacation weeks are too few and ideas such as Sabbath are as foreign as the idea of hibernation. Given this context, if we do tap into our need for rest and care, we are at risk for seeming a bit crazy—crazy for wanting time off and for wanting a sense of spaciousness in our lives. To choose to live life in a way that supports our needs takes considerable determination and the courageous ability to set boundaries. Sometimes, it can seem like a gesture of activism—this art of reclaiming one's life and forming it into a shape that fits us and offers us genuine well-being.

I recall a teaching story shared by Ram Dass in which he talks about a man going to a tailor to get a suit made and when he picks up the suit it doesn't fit at all. One arm is too long, one arm too short; the back is uneven. "Oh no, it fits fine," the tailor says. "You're just wearing it wrong. Here, if you just slump your body over to the side and walk with one arm hanging lower, it fits you perfectly."[1]

This is often how we are encouraged to adapt to the circumstances around us. We mold life into a form that is grossly off-balance, but we don't always see this clearly because those around us don't seem to notice—or they've gotten their suits from the same tailor.

In truth, our wiring is much more closely aligned to the seasonal rhythms we see in nature than our culture would have us believe, with its long work shifts and artificial lighting. Given this reality, we can learn something from the ways of plants, including trees. We can watch them come forth with spring blooms and grow larger in the summer. In the fall, we can see them release the ripened fruits and leaves that are no longer needed before resting back into the stillness of winter.

For many of us, the art of deeply taking care of ourselves depends on a similar type of rhythm, even if this cycle occurs within the course of a day or a week, as opposed to a whole year. Often, we need to find ways to slow down and take breaks. Otherwise, it's nearly impossible to continue showing up in the world with vitality and clear thinking. Although it would be convenient if we could be solar in our nature, consistently rising and shining brightly, for many of us our energy levels wax and wane much like the moon.

A lot of my work as a psychologist involves helping people see these rhythms and consider what it would be like to honor them instead of assuming that their existence is an error. Often, such encouragement is unfamiliar and radical to my clients' ears and psyches. My words are met by some puzzlement, followed by a sense of relief and hopefulness that maybe it's possible to work *with* ourselves as opposed to being at odds with the fundamental nature of who we are. It's worth considering how such rhythms exist in your own life. When have you noticed their presence, and how have you responded to them or ignored them? The following practice offers some questions and an experiment. As with each of these sections, consider this as an invitation to try out some new behaviors and to reflect on these questions by thinking about them, writing about them, or talking them over with someone else—or even with a small group.

Practice

- Begin to listen to and notice how your body and soul want you to live. What are they craving most, and what are some small (and maybe not-so-small) ways you could honor this?

- Are there places where you get stuck in the movement between *engaging in the world* and *turning within?*

- How might you honor this movement between rest and activity, bringing forth new life and releasing what is stale? What would this honoring look like in your daily, weekly, and monthly life?

- Experiment in this next month by making small changes and seeing which ones have the biggest impact on your well-being.

THE ART OF SLOWING DOWN

So much time and so little to do.
Wait a minute. Strike that. Reverse it.

— WILLY WONKA

One key to honoring our rhythms lies in learning how to slow down. I have a friend who's in the middle of a well-deserved sabbatical. These months represent the first chance she's had in two decades to unwind a bit as a working, single mom. "It's just incredible," she remarked, "having time to exercise and read and cook meals and walk outside—it's really unbelievable."

"I'm curious," I asked her. "What's the best part: the exercising, the reading, the cooking, or the walking?"

Without hesitation she replied, "Just having time— that's all. I've never gotten to slow down before, and it's liberating."

Although few of us are graced with the chance to have a sabbatical, most of us could greatly benefit from the opportunity to have more space and time in life so that slowing down could be an option. We live in a culture of speed, and although I've always known this, it became especially apparent to me several years ago when I traveled to Bali.

Within the first day of being there, I found myself awestruck by the Balinese pace of life. I watched them as though they were some rare species, feeling puzzled by the sight of humans moving without rushing. I had never seen people engage in daily tasks without a sense of needing to get on to the next thing.

It also became apparent that they didn't seem to worry in nearly the way I was accustomed to seeing. As opposed to holding tension in their bodies, they carried a quality of lightness and a radiant smile. I commented to a Balinese priest about how people in our country tend to pray, and then worry, and then continue rushing in response to their worry—but people in their country seem to just pray. He confirmed my sense that they actually trust in their prayers.

I realize that my fascination with the Balinese lack of rushing and worrying is based on my own life story. From a young age, my mind has known how to worry and my body has known how to rush with impeccable skill and familiarity. I would say that I was born with these abilities, but I know that technically this isn't possible. Maybe it's more fair to say that somewhere between my first breath and the time I graduated from elementary school these ways of being had become second nature. I could perform them with the ease of a rodeo cowboy spinning his lasso in all directions and with the automatic reflex of a short-order cook flipping dozens of burgers on a grill. My successes at speed were rewarded from a young age: setting records in the 50-yard dash and bringing home certificates that boasted of how many times I could jump rope in ten minutes. I excelled at speed-reading and quickly learned that the faster I got homework done, well, the faster it got done.

Even while being on vacation in Bali, having no need to be in a hurry, I found myself still feeling like a rusher in contrast to these people. Our first night out to dinner, as we were finishing our desserts, my husband asked for the check. Our waiter paused and turned to us with a puzzled look on his face. "Why you in such a hurry?"

My first thought was, *Because, sir, this is what my people do.* But instead of speaking these words, I shrugged my shoulders and half-motioned to our children as though they were the root cause.

I realized how adamant I was to protect the Balinese pace of life as we were driving to the airport to leave the island. We passed a billboard for McDonald's that read: "Buru Buru?" and showed a picture of a cheeseburger. The presence of the restaurant, alone, felt wrong to me, but then I made the mistake of asking our taxi driver, "What does *buru buru* mean?"

"Ahh," he said. "It means 'in a hurry.'"

I screamed, "No!" so loudly that I startled him. "Don't let them take over your land. No *buru buru* . . . resist the *buru buru!*"

I realize that my passionate outcry came from knowing the sort of suffering that comes from rushing and experiencing how hard it is to convert to being a nonrusher once the art of moving quickly has been perfected. For me, it's an ongoing journey of catching myself when I'm moving too fast.

Many people come to my counseling office because they feel overwhelmed by the rushed pace of life. Often, their eyes well up with tears as they sit down on my sofa, simply because they have a rare chance to slow down and be present with themselves. Whenever I leave people alone for a minute or two as I'm getting them a cup of tea, their response is even more notable when I return. Along with the arrival of tears, there's an arrival of wisdom. It's almost uncanny the level of clarity that emerges from simply sitting down for several minutes.

One day in my office, Susan realized that she could no longer live life as the race it had become. "I feel like I'm rushing around all day. My physical therapy clients are booked back-to-back with hardly a break to go to the bathroom, and then when I leave the clinic to pick up my kids the second half of my racing begins. On top of this, when I finally get home I still have paperwork to finish from my workday."

We talked about how she might slow down. Could she afford to see one less client a day, in order to build in time for paperwork and a few small breaks? Was there a way she could use her time in the car as some version of a time-out?

In order to consider these changes, Susan first needed to explore what personal beliefs might be motivating her to rush around and overfill her schedule. For many of us, busyness comes not as a natural outcome of having a lot to do but rather because we've taken on some belief—either consciously or unconsciously—that we're only important and valuable if we're busy. For others, keeping busy may be a strategy for not feeling underlying pain or anxiety or facing the quality of emptiness that can lie beneath the busyness. For Susan, it helped to see that she associated busyness with success. She saw that part of what motivated her to create a jam-packed work schedule was a hope that she would finally receive approval from her hardworking father.

In seeing how these beliefs had been driving her behavior, Susan felt more freedom to begin making some changes. She experimented with scheduling one less client on two weekdays. She also started playing classical music while driving to pick up her kids, as opposed to using this as time to get caught up on the news. She found that these small changes made a big difference. "After experiencing what it was like to slow down and actually enjoy my workday, I realized that it was worth scheduling every day this way. My financial loss from those five clients is a small price to pay for how much better I feel."

Students in the university classes I teach experience the same thing when they slow down. In our courses on spirituality and health, we build in many hands-on practices to have students experiment with bringing their attention to their breath and slowing their pace of walking and talking—giving them time to notice what's around them. For most of these students—no matter their age, faith, creed, or color—this is the first time they've been encouraged to pause. Not surprisingly, some of them receive suspicious responses from their friends, being questioned as to why a person would choose to walk slowly or sit down on a bench without doing anything else.

Skeptical responses aren't the only challenge to slowing down. For all of its benefits, it can feel remarkably difficult to put on the brakes. One reason is that we get so little practice at the skill of shifting our pace that it can feel hard to change our momentum. If we're moving quickly, the thought of slowing down can feel like it requires the energy of turning a train around. I saw this when my husband worked at a nonprofit organization that encouraged employees to take 20 minutes to be quiet, right in the middle of their workday. When he first started working there, I was struck by the employees' good fortune to be given such a rare opportunity. Interestingly, few people ever took advantage of it. Even though some of the individuals were committed to the idea of slowing down, the inconvenience of doing this right in the middle of the workday was prohibitive.

So even when slowing down is encouraged, the demands of everyday life can make it difficult. This is true not only with work obligations but also with personal responsibilities. Even the fun and joy that comes with having a wonderful family and supportive friends can get in the way of slowing our pace. My latest reminder of this was a calendar I purchased for our family refrigerator. I thought the pictures of statues and bamboo shoots might help me feel more balanced and peaceful as I filled in each day's box with our family's activities.

One month included the quote: "Nature doesn't hurry." At first, the words inspired me, and I thought I might pass them on to others. However, as time went on, I felt like the quote was mocking me. It seemed that each time we encountered each other it was pointing out the contrast between nature and me, waving a scornful finger at my quick pace. It made me feel somehow *unnatural* in my way of living, as though there were something fundamentally improper in how I went about yanking open the refrigerator door and grabbing food for breakfast and dinner. Finally, one day, I decided to add a comment just underneath it: "Nature doesn't have kids and a job."

After writing my rebuttal, I felt better immediately and realized I could do the same with other quotes on the calendar.

> There is more to life
> than merely increasing its speed.
> — Gandhi

"True, and once I catch up to it, I'll find out what that is."

I mention this only to offer an honest perspective, because if it were always easy to slow down, we'd all be better at it. I know for myself, when I move slowly through the day life feels more magical. I'm more present with myself and with those around me, and in this way I feel more available to life itself. In contrast, when I fall back into rushing I see how I'm a lesser person for it. I end up bringing to the world exactly what the world doesn't need more of.

It's a complicated journey to change our ways. It can also be challenging to acknowledge when we're the ones responsible for our frenzied pace—much as we might like to blame it on some external force. By observing ourselves, with honesty, we become more aware of the ways in which we choose to rush and how we may be perpetuating a culture of rushing in the world around us. I came to see this, with great humility, when I noticed that along with encouraging my children to move at a slower pace, I was often the person desperately demanding that they rush.

"Hurry up. We're going to be late."

"Speed it up. You're gonna miss the bus."

"Can you move it along a little faster? It's past your bedtime."

"Buru buru! Buru buru!"

In these moments, I can sense how I'm passing on the same seeds that were planted in me and in so many of the people with whom I work. Over time, these reasonable requests to move faster create rushers. They shape the harmful habits that allow the demands of time to pump through our hearts and course through our veins and live in our muscles. Sometimes we forget that by packing in even *positive* activities at a pace that's not feasible we make the act of commuting from one thing to the next a setup for stress.

This awareness in my own life has motivated me to practice the art of slowing down more regularly. I've come to find, along with many of the people with whom I work, that the more we use this skill of downshifting—the more we flex this muscle, even in our imperfect ways—the easier it becomes to access this ability in day-to-day life. I've found this poem, by Mark Nepo, a helpful reminder of the importance of slowing down:

Written While Running

Sometimes I move so fast it hurts.
Though the things coming at me
    are not moving at all.
They are soft and inviting. It's
    approaching them as if they will
    vanish that makes them sharp.
Running into any point
    makes it a knife.[2]

Practice

- Are there beliefs you carry about the necessity of being busy that are getting in the way of slowing down? Reflect on any messages you might have picked up about busyness being associated with success or worthiness. What do you fear would happen if you slowed down? Which beliefs and fears are you ready to let go of?

- Reflect on your relationship to rushing. What changes do you want to make? Are there certain tasks or times of day that might be worth moving through at an intentionally slower pace? What would help you to shift gears even if only for an hour?

- Experiment with the art of slowing down—find one activity each day that you can intentionally do at a slow pace. Try eating a meal slowly, or next time you drive somewhere take your time as you walk from the parking lot to the building.

Take time to notice what it's like to move at this pace. What do you notice that would have gone unseen, untasted, or unheard on another day?

50 Ways to Take a Break

. . . And you—what of your rushed and useful life? Imagine setting it all down—papers, plans, appointments, everything—leaving only a note: "Gone to the fields to be lovely. Be back when I'm through with blooming."

— Lynn Ungar

A great way to help ourselves remember to slow down is by taking time-outs. It's always struck me as a shame that this practice is only considered relevant for young children. I can think of many moments when my children were younger, and even now, that I would give anything to be put in a time-out. *Yes, I'd love to go sit in the corner right now and have no one talk to me. Go to my room and take a nap? Sure thing!*

The beauty of such time-outs became clear to me when my children's naps would overlap and there'd be a window of quiet in the house. I never knew how long this would last, and I came to accept that this unpredictability was part of the experience of parenting young children. At that time, quiet came to be more than a lack of sound. It was the arrival of something deeply restorative and too often lacking. One day, during nap time, I sat down for a minute, closed my eyes, and simply listened. Before having children, I never realized it was possible to listen to quiet. I wasn't aware of how much richness was contained within a moment of silence.

Ten minutes later as my eyes opened, I realized I was sitting amid dozens of puzzle pieces, building blocks, and leftover bits of breakfast that had been scattered around the carpet. Jokingly, I imagined that the army of plastic dinosaurs surrounding me was somehow protecting my sacred space. In truth, their presence was a reminder of how greatly my current life stage differed from the previous one. How much rarer it was to find even a brief amount of time to care for the needs of my soul. My desire, however, to have such moments was as great as, if not greater than, it was before I became a mother.

For us, as parents and adults, there are seldom any external voices encouraging us to pause and take such breaks from our life engagements. I love how author Margaret Wheatley captures this contrast in the following story:

> A busy executive was speaking to her six-year-old niece at the end of a particularly frustrating day. She'd spent the better part of the day trying to get a new printer installed. Nothing had worked, and she was exhausted and very frustrated. On the phone with her young niece, she described in general terms how frustrated she was.
>
> Her niece asked, "Did you try hard?"
>
> "Yes," she replied.
>
> "Did you try really, really hard?"

"Yes, I did."

"Well then," said the six-year-old, "now it's time to go out and play."[3]

Taking such breaks can make all the difference in our day. They help us step aside from the busyness of our lives, and they break up the seemingly never-ending list of chores and obligations and responsibilities. Even if you have just a moment to sit down and let go—and even if it needs to happen right in the midst of plastic dinosaurs or other toys—you'll still experience a moment of respite that can significantly change how you're feeling.

Of course, this doesn't always feel simple to do in adult life, and even if we are presented with five minutes or five hours to go out and play most of us don't. Rather, we fill our time with familiar tasks, in part because the challenge of identifying what else we might do seems too complex for our weary brains to tackle.

I see a version of this phenomenon when university students are given a quick break during class. Suddenly every set of hands is holding a cell phone, checking in to be sure that nothing's been missed. Watching the fervor of this texting activity, one would think these students had been stranded on a deserted island for months.

We adults have our own set of challenges when it comes to relating to open time. As a mother of two small children, Carrie felt like she hadn't had a minute to herself for months. She and I strategized how she might carve out some time by calling in a neighborhood sitter and committing to be off duty for those hours. After coming up with this plan, Carrie returned to our next session confessing that she felt paralyzed when the sitter arrived, honestly unable to name a single thing she could do or wanted to do with her free time. "I'm embarrassed to say that I just went to the bedroom and folded laundry while the sitter played with the kids downstairs. I think I've forgotten how to take a break."

Free-time paralysis is humbling because it makes us realize that underneath whatever scheduling obstacles seem to prevent us from having open time we may also feel hesitant to create such breaks because then we might confront feeling disconnected from our ability to lounge, meander, relax, enjoy life, have fun, or simply be. It seems the phrase *when you don't use it, you lose it* has relevance here, although fortunately these skills can be reclaimed with practice.

One of the most helpful things we can do to ensure that we flex our muscle for taking a break is brainstorm a list of ways we'd like to spend free time. In the field of stress management, people are often encouraged to create a stress-reduction plan before they're stressed, so they're not attempting to come up with one when their minds are too exhausted to generate options. With a list of strategies in place, people can grab the best option from the toolbox they've created. The same idea holds for taking breaks. It's best to have a list already generated to glance at and choose from when the time comes—at least until relaxation activities find a regular place in the rhythm of our lives.

Although the act of taking a break seems quite simple and obvious, sometimes there's value in looking more closely at the subtleties of what can, we hope, become a common-sense process. It's useful to notice that when we need a break there's usually a certain quality to our exhaustion—a certain direction in which our experience of too much–ness is leaning, which in turn suggests what types of activities would be most restorative.

Typically, in order to bring balance to our system, we need the opposite of what we've been immersed in. In Traditional Chinese Medicine, this balancing is viewed as fundamental to healing. When the body is stagnant, it needs stimulation to begin moving again; when it's depleted, it needs nourishment; when it's damp and cold, it needs heat; when it's hot and dry, it needs cooling moisture. In everyday life, the same idea holds: when we've been extremely active, we need rest; and when we've been sitting at a computer inside, we need movement outside. Similarly, when we've been in our head with too much thinking, we need to reconnect with our heart and our feelings; when we've been engaged in repetitive tasks, we need inspiration; and when we've been serious, we need some lightness and laughter.

The following are 50 examples of activities that you can put in your relaxation toolbox. As you read through these ideas, consider what it would look like to bring balance to your life with such breaks. I hope this list will serve as a catalyst for you to brainstorm and create your own list of simple and favorite ways to give yourself a time-out.

If You Need Rest, Quiet, or Alone Time:

1. Take a bath: The author SARK's parenting advice, "If they're crabby, put them in water,"[4] often applies to adults as well. You can make an art out of creating the perfect bathtub experience, with just the right candles, music, and scented bubbles or salts. Of course, taking a bath can also simply involve running the water and getting in.

2. Listen to music: With the arrival of downloadable music, it's even easier to find songs that help in relaxing or recharging. It can be useful to have a variety of playlists handy depending on the mood you're in and the type of music you're looking for.

3. Light a candle: One of the most universal gestures for slowing down and inviting in a sense of the sacred is to light a candle. There's something about the presence of light and flame that can be powerful in helping us reconnect with ourselves.

4. Rest with your legs up on a wall: Resting in an inverted position can feel especially rejuvenating. Try scooting close to a wall and then raising your legs and resting them on the wall in a way that feels comfortable. You can also move into a similar position by resting your legs on the seat of a chair. If the floor is hard, put a blanket under your back and a small pillow under your head.

5. Take a nap: As an alternative, and if you have time, go for the classic nap. Even a short sleep, or resting without sleeping, can make a big difference in recharging our energy.

6. Listen to a guided relaxation: Sometimes it can be helpful to have someone guide us through relaxing the body's different muscle groups to progressively release tension and quiet the mind. Listen to samples of guided relaxations to find one in which the voice and the background music feel like a good fit for you.

7. Take deep belly breaths: Allow your belly (diaphragm) to expand on your inhalation, deepening your breath as a means of relaxing. It can help to practice this type of breathing lying on your back, noticing how your belly rises on the in-breath and falls back toward your spine on the out-breath.

8. Let out a sigh: Sighing is a powerful instant stress release. Play with making different sounds as you elongate your exhalation.

9. Turn off all electronics: For all the benefits cell phones, computers, and other digital devices bring to our lives, they have a tendency to become addictive in how they beckon us to check in, respond, and initiate communication. Take a break from these devices, if for no other reason than to know you can.

10. Enjoy a warm beverage: There's something especially nourishing about sitting down with a warm cup of tea, coffee, or even water with lemon. Sipping on a beverage, in a relaxed way, invites us to reflect on our thoughts and catch up with ourselves.

11. Eat a meal in silence: Whether alone or with others, eating a meal in silence allows us to be much more present with our experience. It's refreshing to bring our complete awareness to the sights, smells, tastes, and textures of our food.

12. Sit in silence: Sometimes it can be helpful to simply *do nothing* by sitting down and allowing your mind to come into the moment. Find a comfortable seated position in which your spine is tall and straight. Let your attention rest on the rhythm of your inhalation and exhalation, just noticing the sensations of your breath.

13. Write in a journal: Writing in a journal offers a wonderful way to check in with yourself. Sometimes you may not even realize the questions you're sitting with and the thoughts you're thinking until you pick up a pen and start writing.

If You Need to Get in Your Body, Get Outside, or Get Away:

14. Go on a walk: Never underestimate the rejuvenating power of getting some fresh air and movement. Make it a point to walk simply for the joy of walking. Whether this takes the form of walking for 30 minutes in nature or walking for 3 minutes from one end of your office building to the other.

15. Sit in nature: It's also refreshing to sit down on a bench or on the ground, especially if you're in a place where you can take in the elements of nature through all your senses. Being outside can offer a helpful reminder that our to-do lists and worries are not the ultimate reality.

16. Explore a park: It may be worth pulling out a map and discovering what parks, nature preserves, and even playgrounds are nearby. Visiting such places, and exploring the hidden treasures within them, can be a wonderful way of being outdoors.

17. Go to a farmers' market: Many communities host markets once or twice a week with local produce and other natural and healthy products. Browsing these types of venues can be inspiring to our meal planning and our thoughts about how to maximize ways of nourishing ourselves and our families. It's also delightful to talk with the people who have grown our food.

18. Meander around town: As a change of pace, walk or drive around your town somewhat aimlessly. While we wouldn't typically do this unless visiting another place with extra time on our hands, why not pretend to be a visitor in your own town?

19. Go to a body of water: There's something magical about being outside by water, regardless of whether it's a pond, lake, stream, ocean, or water fountain. The sound of water moving is especially soothing when we're feeling dried up by our day-to-day lives.

20. Fly a kite: I had forgotten how enjoyable it is to fly a kite until several years ago when my children encouraged me to buy one. There's something metaphoric about this version of taking a break, maybe because it doesn't have a particular purpose or destination other than the sheer enjoyment of watching the wind do its magic.

21. Watch the clouds: Lying on the ground and looking up at the sky to notice the shapes of the clouds is another wonderful way to take a time-out. By using your imagination—finding animated faces, wild animals, and other objects—you can get your mind off the worries of everyday life.

22. Watch the stars: Same goes for watching stars— sometimes we forget that the nighttime has a beauty all its own. A dark sky full of stars is a powerful reminder of the larger mystery that surrounds our lives and our planet.

23. Go for a run: Runners swear by the emotional and physical benefits of this form of exercise. Even if you're only able to jog slowly, you might find this type of movement to be useful in awakening and opening up the body.

24. Take a bike ride: Riding a bike is another simple joy that's worth reconnecting with if you've lost touch with the simple pleasure of pedaling fast and feeling wind on your face.

25. Drive somewhere new: When life feels stagnant, it can help to get away, whether this is to a nearby town or some place that requires a longer road trip.

26. Climb a tree: I'm still waiting for the day when I see an adult stuck up in a tree. Why is it always children and cats who let their spirit of adventure carry them away?

27. Do some gentle stretches: You don't have to stretch in any formal way—it's enough to lie down on the floor and listen to how your body wants to move. Even when you only have two minutes to stretch, those 120 seconds can make a difference.

28. Put on music and dance: By yourself or with your kids, this is a great way to take a break by shaking off your stress and moving a little. Best of all, you get to pick the music!

29. Move twice as slowly: As an instant way to calm down and bring your attention back into the moment, try moving twice as slowly as you otherwise would. When we rush, we fuel the perception that we don't have enough time, but by moving slowly we can start to convince ourselves that we're calm and on top of things.

Plus, moving slowly is a much more dignified way to move through our day.

30. Notice your body: It's easy to end up residing in your head and ignoring everything below it. To come back into your full body, do a quick body scan. Move through each part of your body and notice anything and everything about it. Start with your feet and legs, then move to your stomach and lower back, then your chest, shoulders, arms, and hands, and finally your neck and head.

If You Need Inspiration, Entertainment, Lightness, or a Quick Recharge:

31. Make some music: Whether it be with your voice, a drum, or another musical instrument, play with making some music by yourself or with others. You don't have to be a musician to benefit from the creative release of creating sound.

32. Paint on a surface other than paper: Sometimes moving our creative expression out of the box (maybe even onto a box) is freeing. Consider painting on stones, furniture, a large piece of fabric, or any other medium that sparks your artistic juices.

33. Color with crayons: Why not? It's actually quite refreshing to draw with a crayon—either inside or outside the lines. You may look more respectable doing this while sitting next to a child, but don't let that limit your coloring potential.

34. Read or watch something funny: Being entertained by humor is a great escape and a wonderful way to gain perspective on our worries and stresses. It's a delight to laugh, whether the source of humor is a well-written television show, movie, or book. Sometimes on a bad day, it's just what we need.

35. Read poetry: Poems can carry us into a different reality, lifting up what's most precious and shedding a fresh light on our day-to-day experiences. Explore what styles and authors you most enjoy, or look for collections of poems to get a sampling of different voices.

36. Write a quick poem: Whether it's touching or sarcastic, rhyming or not—play with putting your thoughts down into a few select words.

37. Learn something new: Expand your horizons by learning a new skill, exploring an unfamiliar hobby, or simply finding out the answer to a question you've been curious about.

38. Take a photograph: Along with capturing beautiful moments, try taking a photograph of an ordinary object in a way that's interesting. You may be surprised by what you discover from using your camera in this way.

39. Find a relaxing scent: Often health-food stores have sample bottles of essential oils. Find a scent that feels soothing and enlivening.

40. Examine an everyday object with fresh eyes: Imagine that you're visiting from another planet, with no idea of the names or functions of the things that surround you. How might you see these objects differently?

41. Pet a furry creature: Don't forget the simple joy that can be found in petting a dog or cat. It's hard to say who benefits more from such interactions.

42. Buy flowers: Brighten up your day or someone else's day with a colorful bouquet or even one simple flower.

43. Read a book: Visit your local library and get inspired by all the options out there. For a change of pace, sit in one of the library's comfortable chairs and read there for a while.

44. View art: Visit a museum, gallery, art fair, or other display of creative work. It can be particularly delightful to see collections of children's art.

If You Need to Reconnect with Your Heart:

45. Let something go: If you notice old negative emotions gathering dust in your heart, imagine setting them down—maybe with a ritual of sorts. See if you can resist the temptation to pick them back up again.

46. Forgive someone: Possibly the most powerful form of letting go is to release a grudge, whether we explicitly forgive someone or quietly release anger within ourselves. Think of someone who has hurt you in the past, and see if you can bring a feeling of forgiveness to that person or a sense of *letting go* to the event that caused the pain.

47. Call a friend: Reach out to someone you haven't spoken with in a while, or call a trusted friend with whom you can laugh or simply check in.

48. Write a letter: Letter writing is becoming a lost art with the popularity of the Internet, but there's something powerful about putting words onto a physical form that can be kept. Who do you want to send a letter to? Who would appreciate receiving a letter from you?

49. Engage in a small act of kindness: Think of something small you can do to brighten someone's day, and then do it. Focusing on others can create a break by shifting our focus away from ourselves. If someone you know well isn't nearby, perform a random act of kindness for a stranger.

50. Give thanks: Seeing the world through a lens of gratitude can lift our spirits and offer clarity to help us see the blessings that exist in our day-to-day lives. When we've had too much going on, we can sometimes lose sight of what we're thankful for—but often, our feelings of gratitude are close at hand if we take a few minutes to connect with them. A good way to do this is by writing down all the things we're grateful for and keeping the list nearby. This way, we can look at the list any time we need a reminder of the goodness that's in our lives.

If you'd like a free, printable poster of these *50 Ways to Take a Break*, visit www.fullcupthirstyspirit.com.

Practice

- Given the circumstances of your life, what activities would work best for you to take a break?

- Think about how you want to store and access your list of relaxation tools: possibly on a sheet of paper or entered into your phone or another electronic device? For variety, consider putting them on index cards and drawing one randomly when you're in need of a break.

- See if you can plan ahead by sitting down with your schedule and carving out time for breaks in the upcoming days, weeks, and months.

- It's also useful to prepare ourselves to surrender to those periods of time when taking a break is genuinely impossible. Otherwise, we may end up adding more tension to the situation by feeling bad or guilty that we aren't taking care of ourselves in the ways we would want. As Reinhold Niebuhr's well-known quote reminds us, "God, grant me the serenity to accept the things I cannot change, the courage to change the things I can, and the wisdom to know the difference."[5]

In thinking about *honoring our rhythms* by slowing down and taking breaks, it's good to recognize that these rhythms often change throughout our lives. Similarly, we may find the ways in which we're thirsty and what we're thirsty for also shifting. At one stage of life, honoring our rhythms might include lots of activity and engagement in the world, interspersed with only brief pauses to reboot and recharge. At other times, we may feel called to step back from life in more significant ways—turning our attention within to an even greater degree. Although we may not always understand exactly why this call is happening, there's often great value in following its pull in order to find out.

TURNING WITHIN

You must have a room, or a certain hour or so a day, where you don't know what was in the newspapers that morning, you don't know who your friends are, you don't know what you owe anybody, you don't know what anybody owes to you. This is a place where you can simply experience and bring forth what you are and what you might be.

— JOSEPH CAMPBELL

When slowing down and taking breaks aren't enough, it's likely a sign that we need to step away from life in a more significant way. This was the case for Lisa. Although she was making time for the activities that tended to nourish her—regularly attending exercise classes, having coffee with friends, and receiving occasional massages—she felt completely exhausted and disenchanted by life. "I feel like it should be enough when I get an hour here or there, but I'm just not enjoying anything right now, even the things I usually love to do. Plus, it seems like before I know it, I'm right back at home taking care of my son or folding laundry. It's just not enough, and I feel awful saying that because I realize how lucky I am to have my son, and my husband, and my house . . . "

What Lisa most needed was a way to unplug from her daily life so she could deeply reconnect with herself and rest in a way that wasn't possible with an hour break here and there. She was also experiencing a clash between appreciating the richness of her current life and deeply needing to get away from it. I've witnessed this inner conflict countless times among parents, and I understand this dynamic from my own experience as well. In many ways, my enchantment with my friend's yurt captures this predicament quite well. When he described it to me at lunch that day, it made me realize how much I wanted a place to escape to, even though, ultimately, I didn't want to leave behind all the good things in my life.

Strangely, I even have vivid memories of a time in life when I had a sort of yurt of my own—and, odd as it seems now, a desire to get away from it. At the time, I was living in a town house that overlooked a cornfield. It had two bedrooms, one of which I had converted into an office space for my dissertation. There was big sky out of every window—a hallmark of southern Illinois—and unnoticed quiet filled every room.

When I would take walks around the block, I would peer, best I could, into the windows of the real homes. They contained the warmth of families, with holiday decorations propped and dangling from front porches, and lawn mowers tucked in the corners of garages. There were slides and bikes and silhouettes of chandeliers hanging over kitchen tables. I could smell dinner cooking in the evenings, even though the road was too far away for the scent to reach me.

My yearning back then was palpable, even if I wasn't shouting about it over tables in public places. I wanted, so deeply, to reach back into the comforts of childhood and to be offered some guarantee, or at least a subtle hint, that such treasures would await me again in the future. If someone had told me that 15 years later I'd be sitting in a home with shutters and pumpkins and lovely people on the inside and that my response to these gifts would be to write odes to a yurt I would have howled in laughter and disbelief.

I know better now. I'm sure that in 10 and 12 years, when my children leave for college, I'll cry and pack my own duffel bags in an attempt to follow them. I see the trickery when I long for time to meditate and pray and am then tortured in weekend retreats as I sit on a cushion fantasizing about the fun things I could be doing with my kids.

Maybe my needs could best be met by some sort of time machine that could take me back and forth between the days of my life. It could help me taste sweetness in what often ends up being taken for granted in its too much–ness. With a time machine, I could appreciate everything—and escape it all.

In a sense, Lisa arrived at a similar conclusion. Not that she considered constructing a yurt in her backyard or trying to invent time travel, but she did come to the realization, inconvenient as it was, that she really needed an extended period of time to focus on herself. While taking brief time-outs can be helpful in restoring balance in our days, the purpose of them isn't about reconnecting deeply with our spirit or learning more about who we truly are. In order to really come back home to ourselves, we often need an entire day or even several days away by ourselves. When this isn't possible, it can at least help significantly to schedule time each day for a deeper type of self-reflection.

To address Lisa's needs, we decided to have her husband join the next session to discuss the possibility of her taking some time to step away from life. It was important to explore the ways in which he was willing to support her and to look at some of the beliefs that stood in the way of each of them taking the time they needed.

"If I need time away, doesn't that suggest I'm not happy with my life?"

"Is it okay for me to go alone, and not as a couple—what will the neighbors think?"

As we addressed some of these concerns, we discussed what it means to live in a culture where taking such time away isn't the norm. Lisa had to accept that there might be people in her life who wouldn't understand what she was doing, but that it might help if she viewed her two or three days away as a quality assurance that the next weeks and months would be lived with more clarity and happiness. We also talked about how her husband might create his own version of a retreat, and the value that could come from role modeling this sort of self-care for their son.

It's intriguing that within the context of a busy life taking retreat time can seem close to impossible, yet from the perspective of many spiritual traditions such alone time is essential. The meeting of these two realities can feel like oil and water. Sometimes, books on spirituality can make us feel like something's wrong with us to be leading a life that looks so different from that of a monk or hermit. Books suggesting lengthy daily practices and extended periods of silence should also come with a prescription for free birth control or at least an asterisk denoting that parents and working professionals should ignore the first 150 pages of the 200-page book.

It's complicated, however, because when the backdrop of our life is busyness we need alone time all the more—we're just forced to be a lot more creative, and sometimes a lot more flexible, in how we make it happen. After taking several days to be by herself, Lisa came back feeling like she had reconnected with a sense of wisdom and joy. She found that having some quiet time had brought her attention and presence back within herself, back to the place where she could trust what she heard and where she could connect with what felt like a quality of spirit. Taking time to be with herself more deeply helped Lisa feel more grounded in her busy life, making it more manageable and giving her the ability to be more present to her husband and her son, as well as to herself.

The more people I work with and the longer I live my own life, the more I'm convinced that it's from this place of time away and inner quiet that our capacity for feeling qualities like peace, clarity, gratitude, and generosity can be awakened and reawakened again and again. Of course that doesn't mean there aren't obstacles that get in the way. Joyce is one of many people I've sat with who, at first, was utterly convinced that she could never find a way to have time to herself. "Between my work schedule and the kids' activities, it will just never happen. If I stepped away for even half a day, my corner of the world would crumble."

In sitting with such predicaments, it's important to first look at what obstacles might be self-created. For Joyce, it became apparent that she didn't really want to carve out time. She came to see that, deep down, it felt easier to assume she was a victim of her circumstances than to do something to make her situation different. She also realized that she was scared to create time and space because then she would have to pay attention to things that felt uncomfortable. As we peeled back these layers, she was able to recognize this discomfort. "I've been putting off looking at the stress between my husband and me, and being honest about my gut sense that I need to leave my job. I guess I haven't wanted to face these things."

We talked about ways she could structure a day or two by herself so that the time could feel less frightening and more nourishing. She identified some of the reflective and restful activities she wanted to do: writing down thoughts in her journal about her marriage and her work, taking a slow walk out in the woods, napping, stretching, and envisioning how she might approach her day-to-day life differently to find a better rhythm of continuing to listen within.

For many of us, it's important to consider what our ideal version of a retreat day would look like, as well as noticing what it would require for us to justify taking such time away. I've often been struck by how we need a better way of thinking about and articulating the time away that we need to come back home to ourselves. If we had a socially acceptable language for naming, "I'm unplugging today," "I'm on sabbatical today," "I'm going inward today," this would be helpful. Often, when people say, "I'm taking some time for myself," or, "I'm taking personal leave today," the questions that follow suggest that we should be inserting some alternative activity into the day in order to justify our time off: "Do you have a doctor's appointment?" "Are you getting caught up with some errands or yard work?"

I was reflecting on this issue with a friend of mine who was recently in a car accident. She was describing how her recovery has been challenging in all sorts of ways, but that this forced time away from activity had also allowed her to drop into a place of inner peace and rest that she had never known. We were remarking on how ironic it was that sometimes such health traumas grant people both a *permission* and a *language* to step away from life in a way that is healing at a deeper level. We were questioning how people might access such transformation without having to go through a car accident or a serious diagnosis. How, in the context of ordinary life, might we become more resourceful in finding ways to carve out time for this sort of rich inner journey?

Stephan Rechtschaffen, in his book *Timeshifting*,[1] gives a humorous example of just this. He describes a person who set aside retreat time by writing it into his appointment book in pencil. He then found that he would end up erasing it when other things came up, so he wrote it in pen. Still, he would end up crossing it out, so finally he resorted to cutting the page out of his calendar. Such creative approaches can be helpful.

When we genuinely hold the intention to create space in our life, it becomes possible. It may take some time and require making some changes. As with Joyce, we might have to inspect what beliefs are holding us back. As David Whyte so eloquently puts it, we may also need to "radically simplify whatever complications we've arranged for ourselves."[2]

It's helpful to approach the task of carving out time in both rational and nonrational ways. We may need to look ahead in our schedules—maybe even quite far ahead—and literally or metaphorically cut out some days from our planner, realizing that open time isn't going to magically appear on its own. We can almost always find the time, however, if we approach the task of doing so creatively. When we take a step back and make a quarter turn in how we're viewing our situation, sometimes possibilities emerge that can surprise us. It can help to focus less on the obstacles to taking time away and more on our desire for renewal. It's similar to Antoine de Saint-Exupéry's advice: "If you want to build a ship, don't herd people together to collect wood and don't assign them tasks and work, but rather, teach them to long for the endless immensity of the sea."[3]

When I was in graduate school, I first decided to set aside one day each week to nourish myself. I would walk in nature or write in my journal or meditate or sleep. Whatever I chose to do, I encouraged myself not to have it involve crossing off things from my to-do list but instead to have the time be about taking care of myself and deeply listening to whatever I needed to hear from within. Of course it wasn't always easy to be fully present in my day and to not worry about what wasn't getting done, but, with time, it became easier.

Back then, taking that day felt like a radical thing to do, and mainly I kept it a secret. It helped that I was motivated by a wise woman who suggested that spending time in this way wasn't merely selfish but, instead, might actually allow me to offer more to those around me in the long run. She encouraged me that if I wanted to lead a life oriented toward service and I hoped over time to *do good well,* then such days might actually be essential. Of course, such a suggestion contradicted my thinking at the time—I assumed that if we wanted to help others we should do that *instead* of taking time for ourselves. After a while, though, I came to understand her point. Still, it felt like a strong stance to decide that I was going to deeply nurture myself, even in the midst of every external current suggesting that I do otherwise. When such an act felt impossible or illogical, it helped me to think of people like Gandhi or Martin Luther King Jr. who spent hours a day in contemplation at points in their lives. This would halt my arguments of how I wouldn't be able to get my to-do lists done. It would also quiet my fears that this time would be wasted.

Having said this, I can't imagine being able to take a whole day each week to do this type of nonactivity right now. I have, however, found various ways of stepping out of life by taking retreats several times a year and setting aside a day or part of a day regularly. Each of us has to consider what form of time away can work within our lives, being both realistic . . . but maybe not too realistic.

Practice

- What would be an ideal way of stepping out of life for you? Before focusing on whether it's feasible or not, allow yourself to imagine what would best support you. How much time would you like?

  - Would it be structured in one block of time or across multiple days or months? Would you go away or stay at home?

  - What qualities would you most like to experience from this time: peace, clarity, strength, joy, gratitude, rest, others?

  - What activities, or lack of activities, feel like they'd be most restorative?

- Put this description in a location where you can see it, in order to let these ideas sink in. In a week or so, revisit what you've written down and consider what elements of your plan are possible to make happen. Think creatively.

- You might also want to generate two lists, one that depicts your ideal retreat time and a second that names smaller ways you can carve out restorative time in your day-to-day life. While these mini-retreats might be less significant than a full day away, think of activities that would take more time than the breaks you identified in the last chapter. What nourishing things could you do that might serve as a middle ground between a *quick time-out* and an *all-out stepping away?*

- Notice if you're carrying around any beliefs that are getting in the way of making such retreat time possible. It might help to write out any conflicting thoughts you're having. You can also ask someone you trust to help you sort out these thoughts and beliefs.

- How might taking such retreat time help you to be of service in the world in more creative and fulfilling ways?

What Monks and Sages Tell Us

All of the troubles of life come upon us because we refuse to sit quietly for a while each day in our rooms.

— Blaise Pascal

It's both inspiring and somewhat daunting to see that most religious traditions place tremendous value on turning our attention within, regardless of how the goal is named—"Be still and know that I am God" (Psalms 46:10), "Bide in silence and the radiance of the spirit shall come in and make its home" (Lao Tzu).[4] In essence, this inward turning is what spiritual practice is all about—stilling the mind and coming into the present so that we can connect with our inner wisdom and with the larger truth of existence . . . however we might define this. To quiet ourselves in this way, it helps to have a mechanism to work with our attention. Many approaches exist for coming into the here and now, including Eastern traditions of meditation and Christian approaches to contemplative practice. The following tips offer an introduction and reminder of some key ideas that are important to bring a practice of self-focus into your life.

- Choose a certain time of day.

- Choose a place, preferably a quiet spot or a place that can be made quiet.

- Find a way to sit in which your back can be straight and your body can feel relaxed, whether this is on a chair, a cushion, or some other type of pillow on the floor.

- As you sit down, notice how you're making contact with the chair or cushion and see if you can *ground* or *root* yourself, sitting intentionally. Next, allow your spine to lengthen by imagining someone touching the crown of your head as you extend up into their touch.

- Begin meditating by noticing your breath, not just the idea of your breath but rather the physical sensations of your breath. Where do you sense and notice your inhalation and your exhalation in your body?

- As you notice your breath, also notice what it's like to be noticing. This helps in cultivating the skill of *witnessing* or *observing* our experience. It also creates a sense of spaciousness in our awareness, so we're not entirely consumed by what's going on.

- Let the practice be light—don't *try* too hard, but rather allow the process to be as relaxing as possible.

- Remember to be friendly with yourself. It may help to lower your expectations about what you're hoping to experience.

This practice can be done on a daylong retreat or as part of a regular routine you create in your home—or both. If you are creating a daily practice, begin with a short amount of time, like five minutes. As you practice, you can increase your time. Some people find it helpful to meditate once in the morning and once at night, whether this is for three minutes, ten minutes, or longer. Remember that the point of meditation isn't about having no thoughts at all but rather about focusing your attention in order to quiet your mind.

If you find that simply noticing the breath doesn't work well for you, there are other techniques that can be useful, too. As an example, experiment with these other ways:

- Silently counting the breath to add an extra focal point

- Silently saying a word or short phrase (mantra) with each breath to evoke a certain quality

- Using a visualization connected to nature or to different parts of the body

For instance, you can spend several breaths imagining that you're sending down roots through your tailbone and then drawing up nutrients into your body. For the next breaths, you can focus on imagining water showering down and through your body to cleanse unneeded emotions and thoughts. Several breaths can be used to imagine stoking the fire of your vitality and allowing it to expand throughout your body. Finally, as you breathe in, you can pretend you're sipping air—as if through a straw—imagining that you're taking in the spaciousness of the sky.[5]

Or you can focus your imagery on your body. First visualize breathing in and out of the tailbone (to feel more grounded), next the belly (to strengthen the core of your being), then the heart (to open and energize your connection to the qualities of compassion and love), next the *third eye* area in the middle of your forehead (to awaken your clarity), and then the crown of the head (to strengthen and align your connection to spirit).

Over these next days and weeks, play with some of these variations and with different times and places. As with so many things in life, we need to experiment to discover what works best. In Rob's case, his first attempts at meditating didn't feel successful because when he tried sitting for 20 minutes after work he'd fall asleep. We talked about ways he might change his practice, and this led him to experiment with changing his time to the morning, doing some yoga stretches and energizing breathing before sitting, and lighting some incense to see if the smell would help him feel more calm and alert. Rob also found it helpful to set a stopwatch for five-minute intervals as a way of prompting himself to regain his focus and then consciously start his practice all over again. Along with this, he tried keeping his eyes slightly open, especially when he felt tired.

For other people, it's been different ideas that have made a big difference in their practice. It can be useful to:

- Mix up activities; for example, follow a brief sit with some journal writing or a walk outside.

- Create a beautiful space in your home, possibly with some plants or several objects that feel sacred to you.

- Purchase a cushion or bench specifically made for meditation to support you in sitting with good posture.

- Lie down with a bolster underneath your upper back as opposed to sitting up.

- Play some soft music in the background.

- Listen to a guided CD or DVD.

- Have a cup of tea to mindfully sip.

- Find a friend or small group to practice with or at least check in with.

- Find a teacher or mentor with whom you can consult about your meditation experiences and questions, possibly someone you meet with in person or someone you communicate with by phone or e-mail.

Another significant shift we can make with our retreat time is to frame it as being about deep listening. I love how author Annie Dillard captures this idea: "At a certain point you say to the woods, to the sea, to the mountains, the world, Now I am ready. Now I will stop and be wholly attentive. You empty yourself and wait, listening."[6]

This idea of taking time to listen captures a key reason for turning our attention within. For Rob, approaching his quiet time in this way ended up being especially nurturing and rewarding. He noticed a fundamental difference between what it felt like to be *trying* to focus on his breath and quiet his mind and what it felt like using the time to simply notice and receive whatever images or truths came into his awareness.

Changing his meditation practice in this way wasn't entirely easy, however, because Rob realized that he first needed to address some fears that were keeping him from being able to truly listen. For many of us, it can feel frightening to open up to the truth of our lives and to what we might hear when we allow ourselves to settle into a receptive place. As Rob explained, "For me, what's tricky is that I really want to be open to God's will. This has been my prayer for years, but what I've come to see is that I'm scared of what God wants for me because I'm worried it won't be what I want in my life. I've really had to wrestle with my sense of faith and trust so I can embrace what it would mean to listen—because for me this listening is listening to how God wants to speak to me."

I can think of other people who face similar fears, even when they believe that what they're listening to is their own wisdom as opposed to a divine source of guidance. For many of us, it's challenging to listen because doing so can cause us to feel at higher risk for the possibility that certain dimensions of our lives might not unfold as we want them to. In Rob's case, a key dilemma was that he really wanted to be in partnership with someone but for years had felt a strong sense that to fully pursue his spiritual calling he should not make this type of commitment. "When I get quiet, I know that I need to stop putting so much energy into looking for someone to be with. I guess this scares me because I fear that if I don't keep trying a partnership will never happen, and it's hard for me to accept this."

His experience reminds me of Adyashanti's thought-provoking comment that "the role of the spiritual practice is basically to exhaust the seeker."[7] This spiritual teacher's words suggest that, often, what keeps us from being able to relax and open into life is our tendency to be *looking for* or *going after* something—even if it's something noble like a relationship or spiritual truth.

It helps to be aware that, even when we approach our quiet time with these awarenesses and tips and tools, often what we first encounter is the very opposite of stillness or peace. As we begin to observe our thoughts, we realize just how many of them we have, how unimpressive they tend to be, and how the mind seems to jump all over the place like a wild monkey swinging from branch to branch.

In attempting to quiet the mind, it helps to make a commitment toward self-compassion. It's also helpful if we can have some lightness around our likely ineptitude when it comes to something that seems like it should be so simple—*I mean aren't we just trying to keep our attention on our breath? How hard can that be?*

I've heard meditation teachers from the East comment that when they come to the West they have to factor in the degree to which people in our culture tend to criticize themselves. When instructed to *follow the breath,* typical Western students soon dive into an inner monologue about how awful they are at staying focused on their breath, mentally clubbing themselves over the head for their lack of ability. When encouraged not to be self-critical, they often respond by beating themselves up for clubbing themselves over the head: *Good grief, I'm not a good meditator, and I'm not even kind to myself!*

I know for myself and many of the people I speak with that an essential part of the journey has involved accepting the imperfections of our meditation practice. I've always loved Jack Kornfield's comparison that training the mind is much like potty-training a puppy.[8] We say "stay," and the puppy runs off the newspaper. We bring the puppy back and say "stay" again, and once more the puppy runs off. The key is continuing to come back even if our mind strays 20 times. On a good day, we may bring it back 21 times, but even if we bring it back 19 times and then get lost we're still developing the reflex of redirecting our attention back to the here and now.

I've sometimes joked that participating in Eastern meditation practices has helped bring me back to my Christian roots because, on occasion, during long meditation workshops, I've found myself praying, *Please, God, in Jesus' name, make this meditation end soon. Please have mercy on me and inspire the instructor to ring the bell and end this session.*

Even during shorter practices, I've needed to humbly look at my tendency to sit with my body and mind perched forward, ready for my timer to go off so I can move on to the next thing on my list. While this might seem understandable in the context of *just sitting there*, the truth is that this same tendency is what I, and most of us brought up in our culture, carry into our day. This habit of leaning forward and looking forward to what's coming next is exactly what keeps us from fully showing up in our actual moment-to-moment experiences.

This is why it's so important that we practice the skill of stilling the mind and turning within so we can begin to bring this quality of presence and authenticity into our daily life.

Without a practice *outside* of life, it's difficult to change our habits while we're in motion. As I'll talk about more in Shift 4, a primary goal of sitting meditation is to be able to take this same way of being into our activities. We want to be *mindful* in doing whatever we're doing by noticing such things as how our body is making contact with the chair we're sitting on or how the soles of our feet are touching the ground as we walk. As one of my teachers likes to say, the goal is to add *eyes open* to our meditation, meaning that we take the mindfulness we find on the cushion into the greater world.

Practice

- Try out some of the meditation techniques mentioned to see what works best for you.

- Also, experiment with framing your meditation as being about spending some quiet time to simply listen, reminding yourself that you don't have to do anything but, rather, just allow what wants to happen to happen.

- Do your best to bring compassion and self-acceptance to these practices, knowing that the goal isn't to be perfect.

CONNECTING WITH WHAT MATTERS MOST

The more you sense the rareness and value of your own life, the more you realize that how you use it, how you manifest it, is all your responsibility. We face such a big task, so naturally we sit down for awhile.

— KOBUN CHINO OTOGAWA ROSHI

Possibly the most important reason for carving out time to bring our attention inside and into the present moment is so we don't lose sight of those things that are most precious. We can feel a deep ache if we experience a loss of meaning or a sense of disconnection from what we most value. It helps, as a prevention strategy of sorts, to periodically check in with ourselves to assess what feels most real and important and trustworthy—to identify a *true north* of sorts. This solid point of reference for who we are and what we know to be true can help us as we make our way through the ups and downs of life. Often, a way of arriving at this clarity is by noticing what we're most longing for in the depth of our being. Taking time for such self-reflection ensures that we have clarity around our priorities and that we're shaping our life in alignment with these values.

The process of exploring what we desire is much like peeling back the layers of an onion, starting with the outer layers of what we long for and then moving deeper into our heart and soul. I often ask people in workshops to begin by naming what their personality, or ego, wants for them. I encourage them to list whatever comes to mind and not hold back regardless of how small, large, impressive, or unimpressive the desires might be. People often include material possessions as well as successes they'd like to achieve in their careers or hobbies. Once they've jotted down this list, I have them reflect on why they want these things and what benefit or reward they're hoping these things will bring.

Melanie's hope was to receive a promotion at work in order to move into management. "I guess I want to have some greater financial freedom so I don't have to think about what my kids can and can't do. I also think I'd feel better about myself if I'm able to tell people I'm a manager."

As a next step, I asked Melanie to consider what her heart most deeply yearned for and to notice if that desire felt any different from her initial response.

Without pausing, she responded, "A relationship. I really want to find someone to be with in my life. I haven't felt ready for this in the past year since the divorce, but now I think I'm ready."

In workshops, I have participants come back to this question a second time, asking if there's anything else they're deeply longing for. I ask them to notice what qualities are reflected in the things they've listed. For Melanie, she realized that freedom, fulfillment, and love summed up what she most desired. Others in her group listed security, peace, meaning, enjoyment, service, and a felt sense of spirit. I then invited the group to close their eyes and reflect on these words, asking within if these qualities and desires are in their highest and best interests or if they need to be shifted in some way.

One of Melanie's insights was that she wanted to feel love and connection, not only in a romantic relationship but in all her relationships, including those with her children and co-workers. This awareness was important because it encouraged her to make the most of the connections she already had in her life and to not feel as though she was merely waiting for a promotion to come or for love to arrive. She decided to write down the phrase *Love What's Here* on an index card and place it on the window over her kitchen sink as a reminder. Such a gesture is a wonderful way to honor our deepest desires so that we can bring them more fully into our daily awareness as an intention, aspiration, or prayer.

Along with taking time to step back from life, putting these thoughts into a tangible form is key to ensuring that what's precious doesn't get lost in the density of life's demands. Placing index cards in strategic locations around our home, office, or car can be one small step toward creating a portal to remembering what we most deeply want to remember. It's a symbolic way of creating a version of author C. S. Lewis' *wardrobe,* at least for a moment—leaving behind our inhabited world of daily tasks and doings and stepping into a realm that enlivens our spirits.

Along with phrases and quotes that speak to us, soulful questions can also escort us into this place deep within ourselves. Author Judith Duerk is a master of this type of inquiry.

> How might your life have been different if, once when you were young, struggling to fulfill what you thought ought to be done, but afraid that there

would never be time enough for you . . . something had quietly drawn you to go for a walk in the woods?

If you had slowly walked away from the noise crowding in on you . . . until you heard from within yourself, a silence you had almost forgotten?

If, as you watched the dappled shadows on the ground around you, the wind had suddenly stilled . . . and there was a silence so profound that you entered a new sense of time . . . of time stretching out before you?

And you knew that there would be time enough to let your whole life emerge.

How might your life be different?[9]

When I read these words, I feel like I've stepped back in time and am about to enter a circle of elders who are offering guidance. When we come into silence, we can sometimes feel this type of spiritual support, coming either from outside of ourselves or from the depth of our own truth and wisdom. On one occasion, these words arrived:

> *I used to dream of a long-haired woman*
> *who offered me words of wisdom and comfort.*
> *Then one day I realized*
> *I could stop cutting my hair.*

We must find our own portals to these places between the worlds, whether those portals come through formal spiritual practice, the informal meditation practices I just discussed, being in nature, or sitting with a pet. It can also be powerful to engage in some type of ritual, given the sense of sacredness that can accompany such intentional gestures. We may create these rituals at home, outside in nature, or by participating in an organized activity at a church, temple, or other place of worship. It's good to experiment to see what works best: solitude or community, silence or music, or some combination of candles, prayers, sitting, movement, singing, and chanting—whatever calms and engages us enough so that we're able to deeply listen.

It can take years of exploration to find what most supports us and to discover what allows us to feel like we're coming home spiritually. Our doorways may also change over time, especially when we've lived through the kind of difficulty that causes everything we've come to know to get tossed up in the air. I can recall a period in my life in which the closest thing I could find to a true north was the chirping of morning birds. This sound felt fundamentally real to me when the *realness* of other things was questionable. Somehow hearing those birds created an opening, a portal, that comforted me as I was refinding my center.

We all need sources of orientation and reference points through which to locate ourselves in relationship to what's happening around us. Existentially, we also need to know what we can count on. Of course, when the ground beneath us feels like it's crumbling we sometimes have to let go of our steady markers and simply be willing to stay in conversation with the larger mysteries of life.

Christina Baldwin in her book *The Seven Whispers* offers a wonderful example of this process. She describes a time in her life when she didn't know what to do next and how she approached this uncertainty by committing to sit quietly for 15 minutes each morning and afternoon. She spent this time with a journal in her lap and two questions in her heart: "What do you want me to do?" and "How do I need to change in order to do it?"[10]

For all of us, our doorways to finding and reconnecting with a sense of guidance and truth depend on our theological beliefs—or lack thereof. As Joseph Campbell so powerfully illuminates in his studies of world mythology, every culture across time has its ways of grappling with the mysterious questions regarding the larger truth of existence, including where we come from and where we go to beyond our time here on earth.[11]

So, too, does every individual face these same questions. How we approach the task of answering them depends in great part on where we're from and what we've been exposed to. Often, the true north of our family compass provides us with a path that feels right, or, for others, with a catalyst to turn in a different direction. Sometimes our journeys become defined by fear and sometimes, as Jack Kornfield puts it, by our quest for "a path with heart."[12]

On the one hand, we might find ourselves in love with many traditions and reluctant to marry into only one. As Dr. Seuss might put it: "I will not choose only one view, I will not sit in just one pew, I will not wear a cross or fish, or a Buddha, or a goddess holding a dish."

At the same time, we may feel drawn to Rumi's advice to "spiritual windowshoppers" when he encourages them to choose a path: "Even if you don't know what you want, buy something, to be part of the general exchange."[13]

For some, the spiritual journey involves looking to external forms. For others, it's more about having outside things act like mirrors to point us back inside ourselves. No matter what form it takes, the journey itself calls for us to trust in the sincerity of our intention—that our desire for truth will guide us to the teachers and practices and traditions that are right for us.

In her book *Eat, Pray, Love,* Elizabeth Gilbert describes how the Hopi Indians believe that each of the world religions contains one spiritual thread and that these threads are always seeking one another, wanting to join.[14] In my exposure to different religious traditions, it's been interesting to find that they aren't really all that different. Particularly within the mystical aspect of these traditions, there's a shared recognition of the oneness behind all paths. As Kabir names, "The difference among faiths is only one in names; everywhere the yearning is for the same God."[15]

Even across theistic and nontheistic traditions, the intentions behind spiritual practice are notably alike. There is an encouragement to open ourselves to the greater truth of who we are, whether this involves devotion to God or devotion to our breath. Regardless, the practices contain an invitation to step into what can be called the *thin places,* where the veil between *our world* and the larger truth of life is less dense.

Often, our ways of moving closer to this larger truth involve listening within as well as drawing clarity and inspiration from trusted sources outside of ourselves:

sermons, dharma talks, mentors, sacred texts, wise books, holy sanctuaries, nature's beauty . . . to name a few. Sometimes, however, we can also be thrust into a realization of our true north—as I was when I made the asinine decision to ride a roller coaster with my eight-year-old daughter. The experience ended up shedding light on my deep connection to the word *God* as a compass point in my spiritual life. I understand that some people feel uncomfortable with such language given how often God's name has been used to justify wars and acts of oppression. Yet there's something about referencing the Divine through a word that can provide a life preserver of sorts in moments of distress. At least—as I came to discover—this seems to be the case for me.

The incident started when my daughter enthusiastically announced that she really, really, really, really wanted to ride on a roller coaster at the amusement park next to our hotel. My husband hates roller coasters. I hate roller coasters. However, the one place where our opinions differ is in his belief that it would be a fine thing to have her ride with a kind stranger who, supposedly, we would discover in line on the day we decided to take her.

"No way!" I responded. "We can't have her do that. What if she gets scared midway through, and then even more scared because she's riding with a total stranger?"

When I saw the unchanging expression on my husband's face, I added, "Fine, I'll go."

I had heard that the roller coaster in question didn't have any large drops, and this felt encouraging to the voices in my head that continued to debate my decision for the hours after I had made it. *Really, if it doesn't have drops, how bad can it be? It will be fast, but is speed really an issue? You don't seem to mind going quickly on your bike or in your car. And think of all the relaxation practices you know. With a little deep breathing, you should be fine.*

As we began our slow progression through the winding line of people waiting to board, I could feel my heart begin to beat irregularly. I kept checking in with my daughter, hoping she might have changed her mind, but I could tell that her excitement was only growing. When we arrived at the front of the line, I took a deep breath and got into the empty car with its raised safety bar. It soon lowered, and then the car pulled away slowly, in a cruel way that could only be a false comfort for what was to come.

I'm not sure exactly how to describe the experience of the roller coaster jolting into full speed, but what comes to mind are words like *horror, terror,* and *gasping.* At the time, it seemed like my mind dissociated from my body as a form of survival, and yet every morsel of my experience is lodged into my memory so vividly that clearly I was there for it in some way. What I do know is that the experience was far beyond what I could manage, and I quickly realized that there was a worse scenario than having my potentially scared daughter ride with a stranger: it was having her ride with her mother after she had died from a heart attack.

This was when I knew I needed to reach for something beyond myself, my *true north* for such moments of life and death.

"God *be* with *me*!!" I screamed at the top of my lungs. Then, without even a brief pause of silence, I repeated the plea.

According to my daughter, I screamed this phrase more than 100 times nonstop at the top of my lungs, which made me come off as a complete lunatic to the others on the ride—as though I really cared about their impressions. This was part of the description she provided after tugging my limp but, fortunately, living body out of the car and exclaiming how much fun she had.

After the ride, my daughter skipped and I staggered to meet up with my husband and son, and I mumbled about the importance of finding a restaurant with beer on tap—even though I don't usually drink beer with my meals. All I could muster, along with my moans, was a comparison that I knew my husband would understand. "It was like giving birth, but more intense. If right now you gave me a choice to go into labor with no drugs and even no baby, I would definitely choose it over going on that ride."

What I find notable about this experience is that my cries didn't convey the full clarity I feel I've reached in my spiritual journey. I didn't call out, "May I be free from suffering and attachment!" and I didn't shout repeatedly, "All paths lead to one!" Even with my theistic cry, it seemed Goddess be with me contained one too many syllables.

I screamed to God.

And I meant it from the depth of my being.

Maybe it's fair to say that, in our moments of need, we return to what's most familiar, most simple, and most fundamental, even if our thinking mind has progressed beyond this place. We can think we know what we believe, but really we don't know this fully until we listen to our screams in moments of great pain or joy. And maybe, too, we must notice what we whisper to ourselves in moments of solitude. These things seem more trustworthy than what we find ourselves speaking, or writing, or even posting on our Facebook page.

Practice

- What feels like a *true north* in your life right now?

- Has your *true north* changed over time?

- Explore what you most deeply long for:

  - What does your personality/ego most want?

  - What does your heart most want?

  - What qualities are reflected in these desires?

- ◆ Ask within if these desires and qualities are in your highest and best interests.

- • How does your *true north* relate to what you most deeply long for?

- • Are there ways you can support yourself to be in active conversation with these questions?

- • What would help to ensure that you stay connected with what matters most to you?

Along with whatever insights might arrive at unexpected times, right in the midst of our activity, often it's by taking time away that we reconnect with what matters most. Sometimes, we can't truly appreciate the value of such nonactivity without experiencing it for ourselves. I often encourage people to take a leap and carve out some time to turn their attention within, offering assurance that if they give it a chance and decide it's not for them they can always step back into the happenings of life. Often, though, what they find is that this time is nourishing to a degree that inspires them to want to take better care of themselves, not only spiritually but in others ways as well.

FILLING UP

There are clearly times when quieting down and bringing our energy back into ourselves is a step toward inner peace. Yet the most powerful life is not one in which we bring ourselves back to our center when we have spun away from it, but rather one in which we seek to live from that center at all times.

— MARIANNE WILLIAMSON

As we nourish our spiritual well-being through rest and reflection, we often gain greater clarity about other ways in which we can take care of ourselves in order to bring greater balance to the whole of our lives. In this shift, we use the true north we found—the knowledge of who we are and what we most value—and apply it to the practical aspects of our lives. Here we look at creating strength and stability in our lives by focusing on our emotional and physical health.

The idea of self-care is so simple and basic, yet at the same time it can be one of the most complicated journeys we embark on. When I speak on these matters, I find I have to address this paradox delicately. On the one hand, I don't want to insult people by implying they don't know the obvious fundamentals of caring for a human body (like proper eating, exercise, and rest). On the other hand, I don't want to annoy them by suggesting that these acts of self-care can easily fit into an already-busy life. It's tricky. It's also a sneaky topic in that on the surface it can seem quite boring, even oppressive, like being asked to eat only vanilla ice cream or, worse yet, to avoid the ice-cream parlor altogether. However, beneath the *shoulds* and *should nots,* the world of self-care offers a powerful invitation to listen and respond to our needs so we can more fully inhabit the potential of our lives.

It's an odd predicament that people who have considerable privilege and freedom in setting up their lives often end up feeling trapped by the web of demands and responsibilities that surround them. We can construct lives that end up feeling like prisons, keeping us from engaging in the activities that most deeply nourish us. Clearly, none of us intentionally sets out *not* to take good care of ourselves. Rather, we often arrive in this state over time without fully realizing it.

It's a bit like the tale of the frog immediately jumping out of boiling water but not necessarily sensing the danger when the pot's water is heated up slowly. Similarly, few of us are foolish enough to sign up for an unbearable amount of stress. If someone were to offer us a package that contained a sick child, a job layoff, stresses with our partner, and chronic back pain, we'd all have the good sense to say, "No thanks," and jump. But of course, things in life rarely arrive together, nor are they accompanied by an operator's voice giving us the option to "accept or reject."

It doesn't help matters that we're often encouraged to disregard caring for ourselves or even listening to the basic clues our bodies give us. As children, we are directly wired to our body's needs. If we don't receive food within a certain period of time, we cry; when we need to release waste from our bodies, we poop; and when it comes time to sleep, we close our eyes. There's a simple relationship between what the body needs and how the body responds to those needs.

As we get a bit older, we start to learn that ignoring our body's messages is a necessary part of fitting in and succeeding. It behooves us in kindergarten to learn to wait until a bathroom break to pee and to wait until lunchtime to consume our peanut butter and jelly sandwich. Later in elementary school, we're rewarded for not listening to our body's desires to move. In college, we're helped even more if we can resist this urge for hours on end, perceiving our restlessness or tiredness as cues to drink coffee.

Like so many others, I obtained my black belt in ignoring my needs. I mastered deafening myself to the messages of my body, and in moments when some signal was loud enough to break through I successfully dismantled the connection between listening and responding to what I heard. I felt a sense of accomplishment in my ability to pay no heed to my body's requests for sleep or downtime. Once, in graduate school, I even sat through a class while an ovarian cyst ruptured in my abdomen. Granted, I didn't know what was happening, but it seemed a reasonable option to adjust my body into a less painful position in order to continue with what I was doing.

Curiously, my willingness to not listen to my body wasn't motivated by anything particularly crazy or unusual. It was simply what I understood to be required if I wanted to accomplish good things in the world. It was the formula of *work hard, play hard* that I assumed was necessary in order to fully show up in life. For whatever reasons, what I had perceived as a child were two mutually exclusive paths that could be traveled: that of successful people who offered something significant to the world through hard work and constant busyness and that of the underachievers who took care of themselves because they had nothing better to do. In my confusion, the road I chose felt somehow closer to God. I saw it as the holier path of accomplishment, as though God Herself were pulling the reins and nodding with approval as I did more and more at the cost of my health.

I wish I were alone in this experience, but unfortunately this type of disconnection from ourselves is an epidemic coping strategy for functioning in our world today. Although we can sometimes get caught in exceptional circumstances that make it literally impossible to tend to our needs, more often what happens is something similar to my predicament. Without realizing it, we carry around certain beliefs that prevent us from taking care of ourselves. These beliefs can stem from our family of origin, a religious ideal, people we've admired, the media, or some combination of many sources.

Todd came into counseling after his wife had moved out of the house and his already-present headaches worsened into migraines. It wasn't until then that he saw how ignoring his family life and his body was no longer an option. "I guess I got lost in my work, forgetting that other things in life need my attention as well. But this is how my dad was with the hours he worked—I guess I grew up thinking that this was required in order to be successful."

Jan came to recognize that, for her, avoiding self-care was a response to having a mother who had been extremely self-absorbed and inattentive in her parenting. "I think I just wanted to be the opposite of her. She was so much more concerned with her own activities and dating relationships than us. God forbid that picking up her children might get in the way of getting her nails done. I think I've been concerned that if I take any time for myself, I might become like her."

Kim had made a similar decision in reaction to her husband's behavior. "He takes so much time for his own hobbies from hunting to golfing to playing poker with the guys, it doesn't leave any time for me. If I started to take time for myself, who would cook dinner? Who would help the kids with their homework? I've just surrendered to the situation because it's not worth arguing about."

Both women needed to see that their choice not to take care of themselves as a reaction to someone else's extreme behavior was really only hurting them. In Jan's case, she began trusting in her ability to balance self-care and caring for others as she came to see that there really wasn't the slippery slope she had imagined. For Kim, it helped to strategize how she could talk with her husband about ways they could both carve out time to take care of themselves. In doing this, she needed to acknowledge and let go of her role as martyr. She had to question her assumptions that her husband had no interest in her well-being and that it was somehow her destiny to carry the full load of family responsibilities.

Kara had different reasons for avoiding self-care. She gave up on making such efforts because she got tired of all the mixed messages she'd received about how to be healthy. "First they say eat carbs, then only protein, then red wine, then not too much red wine, then soy, then not soy. I'm sick of following all the changing rules. It also seems nuts to me when I go to a health club and see people lined up on treadmills with headphones in their ears, all staring at TV screens—good grief."

It helped to validate the points Kara was making, and I encouraged her to consider what she wanted to do with these reactions. Did she want to continue sitting out of the health movement altogether, or did she want to use her experiences to inform a better way of making choices for herself? We even talked about how she might help other people sift through the wilderness of information that's out there through a blog site or at least postings on her Facebook page. Certainly, she wasn't alone in her experiences and frustrations.

Another common self-care belief worth questioning is the feeling that *so-so* is good enough. In holistic health classes, I present a ladder of well-being and point out that in our culture we often consider the midpoint, which represents a lack of clinical symptoms, to be the target for health. We can forget that there's a whole top half of the ladder, reflecting various degrees of wellness and vitality over and above merely not being sick. We can also forget that optimizing our wellness is equally relevant if we have a chronic health condition. In the realm of physical health, this upper quadrant of wellness is often tackled by complementary and alternative health practitioners, as well as proponents of fitness and healthy eating. In the realm of emotional and mental well-being, it's captured in the birth of the field of positive psychology. As Christopher Peterson points out in his comprehensive textbook, "Positive psychology is the scientific study of what goes right in life." It's based on the premise that "what is good in life is as genuine as what is bad and therefore deserves equal attention . . . "[1]

While the human tendency to focus on what's wrong has led to many exquisite songs and poems, it behooves us to develop an equally articulate vocabulary around the moments in life when things go well. Such shifts in our thinking can motivate us to live from this upper quadrant of health and vitality.

In applying this idea to our own lives, it's useful to consider the image of a fuel gauge and to reflect on the place from which we operate in life. Is our tank usually more than halfway full, or do we tend to move through life at near empty? At what point do we tend to fill up, and how do we know when we get to this place? Of course, as we are humans, there is no yellow light that comes on to warn us when we only have 20 more miles in us. Instead, we have to figure out our own indications of when it's time to fill up.

Personally, I used to have no problem running my fuel tank down near empty when I was a student. I'd often have only a few drops of fuel left by the time finals came around, but then I could easily refill my tank with a week off from school. Things shift, however, as we reach middle age, and they shift when we have families and work commitments that don't allow us the luxuries of sleeping in and taking naps.

I've heard that in the first year of having children a parent loses an average of 1,000 hours of sleep. When I multiplied this figure by two children it helped me understand that my entry into motherhood hadn't emptied my fuel tank in one fell swoop; rather, I had earned my exhaustion hour by hour. My tiredness became apparent to me when both my children were toddlers and I realized my daydreams of going to a spa were really more reminiscent of a hospital stay.

Oh, it would be so nice if I could just ring a bell for service (nurse's bell?) and be wheeled around so I didn't have to walk (on a gurney?) and not have to make meals and feed myself (IV tube?)—sigh . . .

I wish I could say this was the only indication of my tiredness; however, the parenting offered to my second child during these years was another clear sign. My daughter's bedtime routine was shockingly different from her older brother's. It was the epitome of the different types of attention first and second children get. All that our older child ever knew was a 45-minute bedtime routine that included a snack, a beverage, multiple books and made-up stories, an elaborate series of hugs and kisses, and music played on his personal boom box. In contrast, our daughter's bedtime routine was approximately four minutes long. It's as though our son flew first class every night (the first class of yesteryear) and our daughter was stuck in the economy section back by the toilets. We'd put on her pajamas, offer her a stuffed animal, place her in her crib with a kiss and hug, and wave, saying, "Good night, we love you."

There was a particular day when I realized that I was completely out of gas given my inability to cope with the small and typical hassles of daily life. As I was getting ready for work, I was unable to find the left shoe that matched the shoe on my right foot. In an attempt to locate it, I began crawling underneath the hanging clothes in my closet lamenting, "Where's my shoe?! I need my shoe. It goes with the shoe on my other foot, and they match the outfit I'm wearing. Where's my shoe?!"

Even with only two functioning brain cells, I could sense that my words and my whining were utterly pathetic. My husband, the sweet man, even began looking for the shoe, probably out of a deep knowing that an attempt to redirect my focus to a different pair of shoes or a different outfit would have been risky.

The experience caused me to face the reality that we humans really do have basic needs—that it's not possible to simply transcend sleep and jump to the upper regions of Maslow's hierarchy. It caused me to revise some of my lectures on the mind-body-spirit connection, realizing that although these life dimensions do influence one another, including the mind's effect on the body, that doesn't mean we can override the powerful realities of our physical needs.

Even when we follow the perfect formula for self-care—eating well, exercising, taking vitamins, spending time with friends, praying, thinking happy thoughts when possible—this doesn't always mean we'll perpetually reside in the upper quadrants of health.

I remember how true this was for me in the months before my mother died from cancer. I was in such grief that I had some version of a head or chest cold every day for six months. Although I was doing everything I could to take care of myself, I simply had to surrender to this and chuckle about it with my university students, who had to sit through an entire semester of listening to a sick professor lecture about health.

The reality is that sometimes our best equations for health flow perfectly, and sometimes they fail miserably—it's a reminder that none of us has complete control over our well-being. It helps to embrace a balanced view that we can do what we can, accepting that there will always be variables, known and unknown, that we can't control or even understand. Even in its imperfection, it's still worth doing what we can to maximize our health and vitality.

Practice

- Take some time to reflect on your beliefs and attitudes toward self-care.

  - Where did these beliefs come from?

  - Do these beliefs support you or hinder you?

  - Are there any that you want to revise?

- What would it look like and feel like to deeply take care of yourself?

    - Imagine yourself living in and from this upper quadrant of health and vitality.

    - How can you find a balance between doing what you can to care for yourself and realizing we can't always be successful at such attempts?

- Consider the fuel gauge metaphor:

    - At what point do you usually fill up by taking care of yourself?

    - How low can you safely let your fuel line get?

    - Has this changed over time?

    - What are the signs that you've reached this point?

Seeing What's Most Essential

In pursuit of knowledge, every day something is acquired.
In pursuit of wisdom, every day something is dropped.

— Lao Tzu

To effectively pursue self-care, we must home in on what's most essential to sustain our well-being. We all need to find our own ways of doing this. One of my friends puts sticky notes around her home that read: "What's most essential now?" This is her mechanism for keeping her eye on her priorities, which might otherwise get lost amid the number of demands continually arriving at her metaphoric doorstep. A colleague creates a list of ten essential things she wants to remember and reads this daily.

As we consider the multifaceted nature of day-to-day life, it becomes clear why sticky notes and short lists can be so useful. When exploring these aspects of our daily lives, I find it helpful to conceive of these facets as being slices of a pie. For example, one way to carve up the dimensions of life is into these six areas:

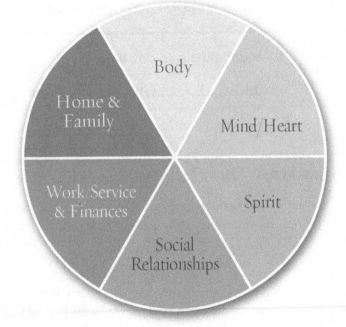

I use this chart as part of an exercise I facilitate with the students I teach. To do it, make two copies of this pie (or your own version of it). On the first copy, color each slice to reflect *how important* this life domain is to you. Start at the center, coloring farther out toward the perimeter for the areas of life that you most value. Set this pie aside and begin coloring the second copy, this time reflecting *how much time and attention* each domain of your life gets. Compare the two pies and notice where discrepancies exist—these suggest the areas of your life where you could use some sticky notes or other reminders.

Given that we only have a limited amount of time and energy, it isn't possible to have every slice fully colored from center to edge, nor is it necessarily a goal that our pie or wheel be perfectly round and able to roll. What's helpful, however, is that we revisit this type of reality check from time to time to see if we're currently living our life in a way that's consistent with what we most value. For me, I do this exercise to see if I'm applying the best of my common sense to my daily decisions. For example, I know that getting rest and eating well are good for me, but I sometimes lose sight of this fact and need a reminder to actually implement my own good advice.

It's also useful to mentally check in with ourselves using a visual like this, given the reality that when we spend time on one aspect of our life we're likely to ignore other aspects. For most people, finding balance in life involves a fluid movement back and forth between various facets of their lives, requiring more of a juggler's agility than the capacity to land in some illusionary place of balance.

Another useful process that I encourage with clients and students is to reflect on what I call *optimal points of entry* into this pie. Given that we can begin the day or week by focusing on any one of these areas, it's good to be aware of which activities serve as catalysts for other activities. Ben responded to this inquiry immediately, recognizing that when he made time for exercise in the morning other good choices followed throughout the day. "My morning run gives me energy and clarity to tackle my to-do list. I've also noticed that it causes me to make better food choices because it doesn't feel good to put junk in my body once I've exercised."

For Julie, the optimal place to begin her wellness efforts was also exercise but, more specifically, lifting weights. "I've noticed that when my muscles feel stronger, I feel stronger emotionally. I'm more confident, which makes it easier for me to interact with people throughout the day."

When reflecting on this same question, Tim and Cindy realized that prayer felt most important. "We don't always make this a priority to do first thing in the day, but we'd like to start. It feels like it would set the right foundation for the day—and for the kids, too. We'd like to pray and focus on giving thanks for all we have to help us keep our priorities straight."

Along with considering what priorities should come first, it's also useful to recognize how we should move forward with our health efforts. Just as we need to find what works best for us to quiet our mind, as discussed in the last chapter, our individual wiring also has to be taken into account in approaching any of our self-care efforts. Some of us do best with a *go big or go home* approach to wellness. If we decide we're going to get in shape, it's best to tackle all aspects at once, from what we're eating, to our exercise, to joining a support group and keeping a log of all we've accomplished. For others, it's best to start with one aspect of a health plan and add in other pieces once solid ground is established with the first goal. Perhaps, we start with exercise, adding an extra workout each week, and then a month later we begin looking at our diet.

At times, it's best to be highly disciplined and structured with our wellness routines. I know people who use timers to ensure they meditate a certain number of minutes in the morning and then to be sure they jog a certain distance after that. Others prefer to be more flexible in their approach. One client, Sara, bridges these two approaches. She sets up an exact structure of what she wants to do each day but also decides that once every two weeks she can toss in what she calls a *screw it chip* and simply allow herself to pass on that activity for the day. "I think those chips are what have kept me on track for five years. Without some built-in breaks, I think I would have taken a break from the whole thing permanently."

It's also good to know if we do best by involving others in our activities or by doing our own thing. I've known people who love going to a yoga class but don't ever do yoga outside of this context. For others, their yoga practice took off when they decided to do it at home by themselves. Exercise buddies can feel like a great idea to some people, but others find this idea to be an unnecessary complication because they'd just prefer to do their own thing.

Some people do best when they focus on *adding* something to their daily routine, for example, drinking more water each day or signing up for a class. For others, they're better off when they focus on *omitting* something—maybe not drinking soda or not watching television during the week. In the long run, both approaches lead to the same goal of shifting our time and energy away from the things that don't serve us and toward the things that do—but it's good to know which path fits best with who we are.

When we consider making lifestyle changes with any of these approaches, it's also helpful to check in about our level of readiness. I'm reminded of the classic lightbulb joke: *How many psychologists does it take to change a lightbulb? Only one, but the lightbulb has to want to change.* James Prochaska's research[2] highlights how people move through several stages as they consider making changes in their behavior. As he outlines, the typical five stages are:

1. Precontemplation (not intending to make a change)

2. Contemplation (intending to take action in the next six months)

3. Preparation (intending to take action in the next month)

4. Action (engaging in the new behavior)

5. Maintenance (sustaining the behavioral change over time)

Prochaska's research is informative because he's found that people are best off *starting where they are* and progressing from one stage to the next, rather than trying to leapfrog across stages. For example, action-based smoking-cessation programs are seldom helpful for people in the precontemplation stage. He has also demonstrated that, for people to move from Stage 1 to Stage 2, it's most important that they start to see an increase in advantages associated with making a change. To move from Stage 2 to Stage 4, it's important that they see fewer perceived disadvantages. The implications of this make sense—if I'm hoping to eat more vegetables or quit my bad habit, I'm more likely to be successful if I come to understand all that I'll gain by making these changes and if I perceive the *costs* as being bearable.

This model is particularly useful in reminding us that changes take time. It also encourages us to stay in active conversation with ourselves as we try new behaviors. Certainly, we're much more likely to stick with habits we enjoy or ones that offer noticeable rewards by bringing us closer to being the person we want to be. For example, it doesn't work to avoid certain foods over time if this restriction feels like deprivation. It also doesn't work well to start with an exercise program that feels too intense or too boring. In the end, we only stay with the practices that we inherently love or that we fall in love with given the benefits we experience from doing them.

Making decisions about our health habits can be a somewhat confusing journey in that sometimes what worked yesterday may not work today. As the phrase goes, *yesterday's solutions can become today's problems.* This is why we have to pay attention to how things are serving us in current time regardless of how ideal or desirable they were in the past. This goes for exercise routines, religious affiliations, and committees we serve on. It goes for questioning if total avoidance or moderation is most appropriate with certain foods or beverages. The answers to these questions can change over time, and the only way we can stay in tune with these changes is by staying in honest dialogue with ourselves.

The more conversations I've had with people about creating healthy changes in their lives, the more I've come to see that, along with saying yes to what we want to move toward, it's equally important that we have the capacity to say no to things we can't afford to give our time and attention to. We can feel tempted to say yes even when such requests involve activities that we don't want to do. It's harder still when we need to say no to good things simply because if we don't there won't be the necessary room in our life for the things that are *really* good and for the ways in which we most want to contribute to the world around us.

Tina had spent the first three decades of her life always saying yes to requests for her time. She volunteered for a variety of activities in her community, helped friends regularly, and was available to her neighbors when they needed her. Although she felt committed to being a generous person, she recognized that she was burned out from trying to be all things for everyone. "After my doctor added a fifth medication to my list, he encouraged me to take a look at the option of saying 'no' every now and then. He seemed convinced that my aches and pains and fatigue and high blood pressure were things I could do something about if I wanted to. It's just hard because I don't want to disappoint others."

We talked about ways in which Tina could find more balance in supporting others while also being true to herself. We explored the possibility of her taking a break from such requests for a month or holding off from taking on new commitments through the end of the year. We also decided on some systems she could use for checking with herself before saying yes, to make sure she really had the energy to carry out the request. She played with *sleeping on* some requests, not always answering the phone, and trying out different phrases she could use when saying "no" that felt both honest and kind.

I've grappled with my own version of figuring out when to say yes and when to say no. I recall a particular week when I had an overwhelming number of e-mails and phone calls to respond to, along with a ridiculously long to-do list. I realized that as much as I felt a commitment to being of service in the world, things had gotten a bit out of hand. At the time I was in a writing group and found creating and sharing this tale to be highly therapeutic:

Hi, my name is Karen, and I'm a recovering re-plier. Now, before you say hello back or make some judgment about the vagueness or smallness of my addiction, I need to be clear, that this has almost cost me my life. Let me explain by sharing a dream I had, in which Saint Peter himself paid me a visit.

I could see the gates behind him, although I don't think I would use the word *pearly* to describe them. They were more sparkly, in the sort of way that heavenly things are depicted on Hallmark cards, with the cleanly glued silver-white glitter that adds a hint of shine and a three-dimensional qual-ity. He was on his cloud. I was on mine, which was nearby, but not touching, and in the dream this de-tail seemed extremely important.

"What did you do with your one life?" This was the question he asked me, with just a subtle hint of an echo, like this, "What did you..$_{you}$ do..$_{do}$ with your one..$_{one}$ life..$_{life}$?"

I answered as honestly as I could, based on the previous week, month, maybe even decade. I said, "I've responded, Saint Pete, just as I'm responding to you now." And I looked at him, waiting for him to say something, and then I realized he was looking at me, waiting for me to finish my sentence, not real-izing that I had already made my proclamation.

When the silence became unbearable, I repeated myself, but this time with more descriptive detail. "I've replied. I've responded to every e-mail and every phone message that has ever been left for me." And I continued with a proud smile. "And this includes all three of my phones. My e-mail, well, I've consolidated that to one account, although my in-box often gets full, much as I try to stay on top of deleting messages and emptying the trash ... but mind you, I only delete the messages after I've responded, unless clearly it's some weird solicitation or sex-related thing, and then I think you'd agree that an immediate delete is warranted. So you see, sir, I am a 'replier.' The best damn replier you've ever seen ... or, I mean, the best blessed replier you've ever seen."

In the dream, I stood there, assuming that the gate doors were about to swing open, feeling proud of how responsible I'd been. I mean, doesn't responsible even translate into "able to respond"?

But instead of ushering me in, he said, "Well, Ms. Ginter ... " and then he paused, trying to find the right way to phrase his question. "Did you ever stop to ask yourself if this was the best use of your time? I mean, are you really sure that responding to others was your life's purpose?"

"Well, I was going to reflect on that, but you see there was never time. The time all got taken, because some of the responses were complicated. Some required more than an e-mail or a phone call. They required doing things, you know, like serving on committees."

"So you're telling me that the best action you ever took was to serve on a committee because someone asked you to?"

"Yes," I answered, with enthusiasm, hearing only faintly the groan of the gates pressing closer together, "and I was a really, really good committee member. I always went to meetings, and I made follow-up phone calls, and I ran errands, and I copied and cut and collated things. I didn't even ask to be reimbursed for my personal expenses most of the time. I was—"

But before I could finish, Saint Peter's head started shaking back and forth. There was the sound of thunderbolts and the arrival of more clouds as I began to drift away. "You!" he said, with a finger-pointing intonation. "You are charged with not fully living your life!"

Well, you can imagine the cold sweat I awoke with. I was panicked, because I knew he was right, but I also felt misunderstood. Even though I couldn't see him anymore, I started talking to the ceiling, hoping that the swirls of off-white plaster could somehow offer a portal of communication to the heavens.

"Please, I beg you. I really had started to realize that a life as a replier wasn't enough. Look through my e-mails from last week. Do you see how I'm making them shorter? I type 'K' instead of 'Karen,' and I've stopped replying to thank-you e-mails, realizing that it's just saying thank you to a thank-you and that it could go on for all of eternity—I mean no offense."

In desperation, I realized I'd better dig a little deeper. "I don't even really like all those committees. Actually, some of them I've come to hate, but I've been trapped. It's like I've had some tattoo on my body that reads: 'Ask me to be on your committee!'"

And at this point I broke down into tears. This was a low point, folks.

But by some grace, when the tears were all done, I resurfaced my wet face from my arms, and I spoke clearly and calmly to the Saints above.

"Okay, I can do better . . . I'll be better. I promise. I'll duck behind cafeteria tables so the PTA moms don't spot me as one of them. And I'll really think about what feels meaningful and not always automatically respond to the demands of others. And maybe I can help other people, like me, who give their time away without really thinking about it. I'll use my downfall to be of service."

So you see, this is why I'm here today with you. Because Saint Peter seemed pleased by this. He came back that night, in another dream, but this time he was nodding his head, saying, "Tell your story. Warn others who, like you, might give away too many moments of their life, just out of habit. And if you do well, then maybe . . . just maybe . . . when your time comes, you'll get to see the glitter up close."

Although most of us wouldn't choose to write a quirky tale as a way of highlighting our health priorities—whether they involve remembering to say no or remembering what we want to do first thing in the morning—it's important that we have some way of naming and tracking the decisions we've made to help us follow through on our self-care plans. Consider writing down your responses to the following questions and periodically coming back to review and update them.

Practice

- When you consider the pie slices in your life and the amount of attention given to each, what shifts are you inspired to make?

- What serves as your ideal *point of entry* when

focusing on your wellness—what activity are you best off doing first?

- How does it work best for you to approach your wellness efforts: all or none or a little change at a time, being highly disciplined or more flexible, doing your activities alone or with others, adding something or omitting something? Your answers to these questions will guide you in developing the most effective health plan.

- Look at the new changes you're considering and reflect on your readiness to make those shifts. In what ways will you need to say yes and no in order to make such changes possible?

Understanding Ambivalence

Ambivalence is a wonderful tune to dance to.
It has a rhythm all its own.

— Erica Jong

As we move further down the path of self-care, we encounter numerous crossroads as we continue to assess the most essential ways of filling up and recharging. Not only do we stumble upon these forks in the road each time we set goals for our health but we also return to these places almost every day as we decide whether or not to stick with our commitments. It would be helpful if we could approach these choices with a unified inner voice, if we could feel 100 percent of ourselves standing behind our proclaimed yes or no. Often, however, we experience more than one answer within. We tap into different parts of ourselves, each with a varying opinion about what should happen or what we should do. This reality is in no way a sign of craziness. Instead, it simply reflects the multiplicity inherent to the human psyche.

When asked, "How are you doing?" in passing conversation, most of us answer, "Fine," out of habit and as a summary sentiment. If we were to answer honestly and thoroughly, the response would be much more complicated and multifaceted. We'd have to discuss what we're worrying about and the ways we feel joyful and grateful, along with the things that irritate us.

Often, we bring this same inner complexity to our decision making. A part of us is excited and eager to begin a new exercise routine or to give up desserts, but usually right behind this voice sits a different part of us that finds such ideas to be unappealing or even horrifying.

Carrie experienced this mixture of emotions when we talked about her decision to quit smoking. "I know I want to quit. I know I have to quit. But every time I have a stressful day, I can't stop myself from reaching into my purse and pulling out a cigarette. Honestly, it feels like the one nice thing I can offer to myself after a hard day of working and parenting."

Rachel felt a similar ambivalence around her decision to start exercising. "Here, I have my workouts all planned on my calendar, but when I get up in the morning, I don't want to go. It feels like a good idea in theory. I know I want to lose thirty pounds. But when

I try to convince myself to put on my shoes and head to the gym, all these other feelings start coming up. I feel lazy and a bit scared, and my mind thinks of all the other things I should be doing instead."

For Deborah, her goal was to carve out more space to take care of herself. She realized that, in order to do this, she would have to start saying no to some of the ongoing requests from her extended family. "Because I've always taken care of my dad's finances and cleaned my grandmother's apartment, everyone looks to me to keep doing these things. It's been my way of helping out, but now it's close to impossible with all that I have to do for my own kids and my own house. I feel like it would be healthy for me to simply tell my dad that I can't do it all anymore, but then I get this queasy feeling in the pit of my stomach."

Each of these women needed to explore the *tune of her ambivalence* in order to understand how to reach her goals. Often, within the self-help movement, people are encouraged to push aside their conflicting feelings and to focus instead on strengthening their resolve to change. This warrior-like approach is based on the notion that if we puff up the winning team and beat down the opposition, victory will be ours. Unfortunately, such an approach is unlikely to lead to lasting improvements. More often, this type of unilateral decision results in short-term changes that are approached with initial gusto but then fizzle out. We quit smoking, but only until the next crisis arrives; we exercise devoutly for a week, but then drop our routine; or we say no to certain requests but find ourselves saying yes the next day.

There's a particular approach to psychotherapy that's quite useful when it comes to these mixed feelings. It was developed by family therapist Richard Schwartz in response to his observation that doing counseling with individuals was really quite similar to doing counseling with families. As he joked, the main difference he saw was that with individuals he'd hear conflicting opinions inside of one person, as opposed to between people. His approach to therapy, named *Internal Family Systems,*[3] offers a compassionate and creative way of getting to know the various parts within us. This model acknowledges that we all have parts that protect us and parts that feel the need to be protected. We can also have feisty, rebellious parts that try to keep us feeling powerful or at least distracted from our pain.

As Schwartz points out, within this symphony of parts there also exists a conductor, called the Self. When we strengthen the presence of this wise place within, we can bring harmony to the many sounds and agendas that push and pull within us.

The three women mentioned offer great examples of how useful this framework can be when making healthy changes. For all of them, it was key to see the wisdom in their resistance. Even if the reasons behind their inner *lack of cooperation* were a bit misguided or extreme, these parts had good intentions that needed to be understood before a successful negotiation could occur.

For Carrie, as we explored the part of her that always reached for a cigarette, she discovered that its intention was wanting her to have relief. As she spoke, imagining herself to be this part, tears rolled down her cheeks. "I just think you deserve a break. You work so hard all day, and you're *on* all the time as a single mom. When you finally go off-duty for the night, I want you to be able to relax—and I don't think you really know how to relax without a cigarette." Giving voice to this urge to smoke allowed Carrie to better understand what was going on inside of herself. By *personifying* this desire and imaging being in conversation with it, Carrie lessened the urge, offering her a chance to find other ways to relax.

As we explored the part of Rachel that kept her from getting to the gym, she discovered some unexpected emotions. It seemed that this part was scared for her to lose weight. By staying with these feelings, she realized that her weight gain was a response to being sexually abused as a child. This had seemed like a good way to protect herself from having something like this happen again. It helped considerably to have a dialogue with this part and to reassure it that Rachel was now safe. She no longer needed extra pounds as a protective buffer.

Deborah's situation was a little different. She discovered a part of her that was terrified of not pleasing other people. As we explored her reasons for saying yes to her family members, it became clear that this response came not so much out of a genuine desire to be helpful but more out of a place of fearing that something terrible might happen to her if she weren't good. As I guided her to ask this part where its belief came from, Deborah recalled several incidents when she was physically punished as a child for not doing her chores.

It seemed the trauma from these events had left her somewhat frozen in time, unable to respond in any way other than to simply say yes in order to avoid pain. For Deborah to move into a more empowered place, she needed to learn how to nurture and comfort this childlike part of her. As it began to feel less vulnerable, she felt more freedom to make choices from a place of confidence rather than fear and pain.

It's very helpful to become aware of the parts inside of ourselves that show up as central players in our day-to-day lives. Most often, these same parts are the ones that hold the key to whether or not we end up making healthy changes over time.

One approach to considering the various facets of who we are is to create a visual map of our parts. You can do this by drawing with a set of colored markers, cutting out pictures from magazines, or using clip art images from your computer. You'll want to find images that represent different facets of your personality and create a collage that reflects all of who you are. You can approach this in a number of ways. Perhaps you can consider yourself to be like a gemstone in which different facets shine forth depending on the situation in which you find yourself. You might want to consider what roles you have in your life, what *hats* you wear across the week, what actions you engage in, what emotions you tend to feel, what words you find coming out of your mouth, and what desires you have. Following any or all of these threads will lead you to seeing some of your different parts. You'll also want to include a representation of the centered and clear place of your Self that exists within you as well.

By doing this exercise, you may begin to see, if you haven't already, the parts of yourself that are in conflict with one another. You may even notice parts of you in conflict around wanting busyness in life and not wanting busyness in life. It's useful to imagine your Self sitting down at a conference table and mediating with these parts. What does each part want *for* you? What does each part want *from* you? What does each part wish that the other one could understand? What is each part worried might happen if it doesn't uphold its agenda? Is there a common ground that can be found and possibly some other parts that might be able to help in getting things unstuck?

Practice

- As you have time, work on a map of your parts.

- Notice where in your life you feel ambivalence. When do you notice yourself thinking or saying, *A part of me feels one way, but another part of me feels differently?*

- How does this ambivalence relate to the busyness in your life? Are there parts of you that are fine with busyness, maybe even create it, and other parts of you that want more space in life?

- Try out the conference table technique with these conflicting parts. Be sure your Self is present, acting as a curious and unbiased mediator.

- As you go through your week, notice other times when you feel a multiplicity of responses, especially around your self-care efforts. Remember that this is a common experience and that the more we come to know these parts of ourselves, the better able we are to move toward greater wellness.

The task of taking care of ourselves involves a lifelong journey of listening to our wisdom about how best to support ourselves, acting on this wisdom, and then periodically revising our plans as we change and as our life changes. The more we learn to take care of ourselves—by balancing the needs of different parts within us and finding a balance between activity and rest—the better we can live out our days with a sense of full presence and vitality.

FULLY INHABITING OUR DAYS

There are only two ways to live your life.
One is as though nothing is a miracle.
The other is as though everything is a miracle.

—ALBERT EINSTEIN

When we think of the underlying reason for engaging in the first three shifts—honoring our rhythms, turning within, and filling up—it comes down to making the most of our days. We want to be able to fully show up for our life, in real time—otherwise, these other gestures become pointless. Over the long run, it only makes sense to *honor our rhythms* if we find that such honoring provides us with more energy and presence in our life, just as it only makes sense to *fill up* through self-care if we experience the benefits of these activities in our personal health. The importance of *turning within,* taking reflective time to connect with our spirit, only makes sense if we can then act on this clarity—moving our practices *off the mat* and *off the cushion* in order to live them authentically in our daily life.

While most of us would agree that we want to bring the fruits of our inner life to our outer life, this doesn't always happen automatically. Just as we can sometimes feel the need for some inward time to catch up with our life, we can also find ourselves sensing that our way of showing up in the world needs to catch up with how we've evolved on the inside. Expressing our essence and making a difference in the world are important next steps after having taken quiet time to connect with ourselves more deeply. This expression might take on a subtle form like walking a little taller, feeling less need to qualify everything we say, setting better boundaries, or being more creative and courageous in our ways of offering service to others. It might also take on larger forms like changing jobs or schedules or homes.

In a small way, I see the gifts and challenges of this *return to the world* in facilitating yoga and helping people shift from a place of deep rest to a place of readiness to drive away and return to activity. I encourage them not to leave behind their restful experience but to try to keep it with them while they add on a more alert state of presence. I also suggest that they identify, in words or in an image, what they've connected with that they want to remember as they transition back to their day. This helps create a *trail of bread crumbs* right back to the truth they've found inside.

This same advice holds true for bringing back the best of what we discover during our inward time—it helps to have ways of remembering what we want to remember. It also helps to embrace this re-entry with a certain level of care that we would give to anything precious. Often, the truths that we find when we've had quiet time feel somewhat delicate in their newness. It takes practice to translate them to the outside of our lives. A first step can be finding a safe place, whether this is with one person or a small group of people, where we can speak about what we've discovered inside. The goal of such conversation isn't necessarily to be articulate but rather to experiment with giving voice to what we've found in our hearts and souls. It's powerful to have such words heard by others who can offer a supportive presence, but it's even more important that we let *ourselves* hear our words so that we can integrate these truths into our whole being and into our outer life.

Fully inhabiting our days involves not only giving expression to that which we've found from listening within but also bringing a similar quality of listening and attention to our outer life. Several years ago, a friend told me a story about being at a dinner party. After the plates were cleared from the table, my friend's date stuck her fingers into the remaining stick of butter on the table and started playing with it. As she smeared the butter around on its plate, she sensed my friend's awkwardness *(What in the world is she doing with that butter?)*. Without stopping, she beckoned, saying, "Put your hands in the butter, *put your hands in the butter!*" until finally my friend did.

This moment soon became a mantra in their relationship. When one person appeared to be avoiding something or not fully engaging in life, the other would exclaim, "Put your hands in the butter!"

Ever since I heard this, I've felt inspired to show up in life more fully—not necessarily by getting my fingers all slimy but at least by slowing down enough to pay attention to what's around me in my day-to-day world.

I realize that many of the people sitting at that table might not have even noticed the pat of butter, let alone been drawn to dive into it. However, the popularity of books and workshops on living mindfully suggests that there's an increasing readiness and hunger to learn how to be fully present in such ordinary moments of everyday life.

I have another friend whose current New Year's resolution is to notice a unique object that catches his attention every day. He keeps a small notebook with him to jot down the image and its color, and unlike me—and many others I know—he's actually been true to his commitment. I realize, in knowing him, that his intention isn't to practice mindfulness, nor to capture the miracles within everyday life. I can't help but see his actions in these ways, however, given his daily ritual.

"Today it was a bright red bike with black-trimmed wheels," he told me, when I called to ask him if he thought the things he tended to notice were beautiful. I was curious about this because I often reflect on how it's all too easy to miss moments of beauty when our lives are busy.

"Well, I'm not setting out to see beauty," he explained, "but usually what gets my attention is something that is pleasing to my senses."

Hmm . . . I thought, *just as I suspected.* If one looks to the definition of beauty, "the quality in a person or thing that gives pleasure to the senses or pleasurably exalts the mind or spirit," then his daily practice of noticing could be seen as an intentional act of paying attention to beauty.

The gift of noticing beauty became clear to me several years ago when I traveled to Indonesia. I awoke my first morning to the sounds of strange birds, the smells of exotic spices, and the sights of terraced rice paddies and dirt roads lined with roosters in wicker cages. I was utterly enchanted by the beauty everywhere, in love with this world of new sensory delights. Yet two weeks later, I realized I was walking along the road, stepping around the wicker cages without paying any attention to their presence or to the strange sounds coming from them. How quickly my sense of noticing had worn off as my surroundings faded from novel to familiar.

Since returning, I've tried to make it a habit to pay attention to at least some of the beautiful things tucked in the corners of my everyday world, to see again the versions of wicker rooster cages that exist in my neighborhood and my yard and along my daily drive to work. I've sometimes brought a camera along to these ordinary places, so I can see them through the freshness of this lens as I do when snapping endless photos as a tourist. I felt confirmed in this venture one day as I set up for a yoga class by laying out copies of a quotation accompanied by a local photo of fall trees by a pond. As several women arrived they began commenting, "This is so beautiful. Where in the world is this place . . . ?"

Seeing the familiar from a new point of view can enliven our day-to-day experiences. In a course taught by one of my colleagues, the students took part in an exercise to explore their relationship to nature by visiting a nearby wooded area carrying card-stock picture frames in various sizes. They were instructed to place or hang these frames, however they wanted, to create an interesting piece of artwork for others to see. She then handed out plastic champagne glasses with the mission to fill them with scented items. The students came back and shared their findings, creating an aromatic feast. The students then headed out in pairs, each taking a turn being blindfolded as the other led them to a textured object that they had to feel. Finally, the students gathered in silence and listened to the winds blowing through the crisp autumn leaves.

This opportunity to pay attention was remarkably rich for these students. They commented, however, that this type of noticing requires the luxury of time. I know for myself, there are days when my intention to pay attention only makes me aware of how much I'm just trying to get through my list of tasks. This is a key problem with busyness—when we're in this mode we really don't see anything.

My puppy, Max, has been a good teacher in this regard. When we take a walk, he has no interest in being rushed or any particular desire to make progress on our route, regardless of my agenda. His focus, seen in one way, is to discover objects of *beauty* over and over again. His way of saying "I like this" (instead of jotting it in a notebook) is to carry the cherished item in his mouth for about 20 seconds, until he discards it in favor of the next leaf or stick or pinecone.

Both Max's behavior and my friend's remind me of the notion that *loving-kindness* can be defined as "paying attention." Although I'm not sure that my friend would agree with me, nor would some of the objects that get crumpled and gnawed in Max's teeth, I think the fact that my friend and Max both take time to notice what's around them offers a sort of sweetness to the world. I realize that most of us don't choose to pay attention by carrying a notepad or sniffing our way from object to object. Nonetheless, it helps to have a strategy for showing up and noticing the world around us—some way of encouraging ourselves to step outside the tight circle of our own thoughts.

I sit with many people who now realize that for years they approached their daily life as something to tackle and get through. They were never encouraged to reconsider this mind-set and were never pushed to reflect on what gets lost along the way when life is lived in this manner.

What becomes essential in order to move into greater wellness is to look closely at how we go about doing what we're doing. As Buddhist teacher Sharon Salzberg notes, "The way we do anything can reflect the way we do everything."[1] These words remind me of a cartoon a friend gave me that shows a monk sweeping the floor. Over his head is a bubble that shows what he's thinking. It contains the same image of a monk sweeping the floor. The humor of the cartoon comes from the reality that for many of us, if we were to draw such a thought bubble it would rarely show the same scene we are currently living. When we're sweeping, often our minds are considering all the seemingly better alternatives to sweeping.

Diane realized how challenging it was to stay in the present moment ever since she moved her business to a home office. "I'm constantly thinking about housework while I'm on conference calls, and when I break from work to start a load of laundry I'm consumed by all the e-mails that are waiting for me."

Diane also described how inspired she felt when watching her priest perform various rituals during Mass. "I love how slowly and thoughtfully he prepares the elements for communion and how he spends as much time and care wiping out the silver cups and plates. You can tell it's all very sacred to him."

In addition to strategies like writing reminder notes to put on her computer and her dryer door, we talked about what daily actions she could approach with this same quality of attention used by her priest and how this might alter her way of being in relationship with them. She experimented with sending a blessing to each person to whom she sent an e-mail. She played with folding her family's laundry as though the clothes were sacred, deserving loving care and respect. Diane also decided to get some flowers each month. She realized that she hadn't done this in years and sensed that seeing a vase filled with bright petals would be a wonderful reminder to notice the beauty in her day-to-day life.

It's an ongoing journey to continually bring our mind and our presence back into the moment while we're engaged in life. The gift of this may not be so obvious with sweeping and e-mails and other daily tasks. One could easily argue, "Why would I want to be present for such things, anyhow?" I know I have moments of thinking this when I'm working through a monotonous to-do list. I've come to see, though, that so many sweeping-like moments exist in life—if we don't show up for them, we miss out on a very large chunk of our human experience. Even more so, we miss out on the possibility that these moments could actually become interesting, maybe even a bit extraordinary. When I read the poetry of Naomi Shihab Nye, I sense she's a master at this. As she writes:

. . . So I'll tell you a secret instead:
poems hide. In the bottom of our shoes,
they are sleeping. They are the shadows
drifting across our ceilings the moment
before we wake up. What we have to do
is live in a way that lets us find them . . .
Maybe if we re-invent whatever our lives give us
we find poems. Check your garage, the odd sock
in your drawer, the person you almost like, but not quite.
And let me know.[2]

Practice

- How can you support yourself in bringing what you find during your time within back out into your day-to-day life? What might this expression look like?

- Set an intention to show up fully in this day.

  - What helps you to be in the moment?

  - How does this type of awareness affect your experience of being busy?

- Play with bringing your attention to your senses. Notice what objects visually catch your eye, what smells and sounds surround you in different places during the day. Notice the things that are very ordinary.

- Experiment over the next week with what methods work best for you. Does it help to keep a journal, to carry a camera, to write poems, or maybe to cover your fingers in whatever is sitting right in front of you?

LISTENING TO LIFE

Listen to your broccoli, and your broccoli will tell you how to eat it.

— ANNE LAMOTT (QUOTING MEL BROOKS)

By showing up in life and paying attention, we can sense the subtleties of what's around us and we can begin to hear what the seen and unseen worlds have to say. Sometimes, I think the universe is constantly offering clues to us and that by bringing our full presence to the day we become available to hear them. This quality of listening to the world around us is a powerful gift that comes from fully showing up in life—and just as it's beneficial to turn our attention within and listen, a similar clarity can be found from such outer listening.

When we need inspiration and clarity, it can help to approach the world around us as our teacher. We can look to the people, objects, images, and quotes that come our way as being the potential bearers of some nugget of guidance or wisdom. The natural world is also an amazing teacher, especially in offering lessons about what's required to live a balanced life. It's notable to see an unearthed tree and realize that its roots are as large as its branches, that its system for acquiring nutrients takes up as much space as its vehicle for bearing fruit. The moon offers a different sort of reminder in how light can be reflected as well as generated. There's also the parched soil in my potted plants that at first resists water, not being able to take in what it most needs until it is softened. I imagine these curious realities are offering a certain wisdom to us.

When clients feel stuck about some situation in their life, I often encourage them to adopt this lens of viewing life as a teacher. I suggest that they walk outside, look at everything, listen to everything, and invite the world to: "Show me. Teach me." This inquiry is useful not only when in nature but also when we use it as a frame for reviewing our life experiences from the day or even the year. What have we learned? What has life been trying to teach us? What has captured our attention?

I love how author Parker Palmer captures the importance of listening, not only to the outer world around us but also to the outer dimensions of our life. As he encourages, "Before I can tell my life what I want to do with it, I must listen to my life telling me who I am."[3] His words remind us that there's value in paying attention to the external circumstances of our life and the impact they're having on us, just as we might listen to our inner wisdom during times of solitude and retreat.

Sometimes, imagining what our life is saying to us can help us find clarity when we otherwise feel confused. This was true for Kelly. Her initial attempts at deciding whether or not she should go back to work felt like a dead end. But, when she asked herself, "What has my life been saying to me?" she was able to see things more clearly. She realized that her frequent daydreams of redecorating her home, cooking meals in her kitchen, and volunteering at a local food pantry were, in a sense, messages her life was giving to her. They were showing her not only what she most wanted but also—with a twist in logic—how her life was wanting to be lived through her.

For Kara, a single mother, a similar reflection allowed her to recognize that it was time to end her dating relationship. "When I reflect on what my life's been telling me, I see that I've been trying way too hard to make this relationship work. I think I've worn myself out trying to make him into someone he's not—hoping he'll want to make a long-term commitment and want to show up as a consistent person in my son's life. When I was walking around the other day, looking at the crops growing on the farmland, I had such a strong sense of how things grow more and more into what they are. You can't make soybeans into corn, and I'm not going to make him into someone he's fundamentally not."

This type of listening to our life and to the world around us takes practice. It helps to take a step back, even imagining that we're seeing our day-to-day experiences from an aerial view. It also helps to adopt a lens of curiosity as we attempt to stay in conversation with our life. In a workshop that my husband and I teach, we pass out index cards that have the words *Hmm . . . isn't that interesting?* printed on them. These serve as a reminder for participants to stay curious and open to what's happening throughout their days. The group often laughs as we think through situations in which this exercise would only result in repressing our frustration: "Oh, you got expelled from school today? Oh, you forgot to pick up the dry cleaning I need? Isn't that interesting?" For more neutral situations, however, it's a useful exercise to try out—it helps in noticing how we often react with an automatic and predetermined response rather than allowing ourselves to be present with our actual experiences in order to truly listen to what they're telling us.

One of the reasons I love to write and take pictures is because both pursuits offer permission to get more curious about the world—to practice saying, "Hmm, isn't that interesting?" Writers often carry pens, just as photographers carry cameras, in order to capture moments that are notable, quirky, touching, or odd. When we look through these lenses, very few moments seem ordinary or boring. These artistic tools provide a mechanism for pulling forth the hidden brilliance in life. Having these tools handy also puts us in the mind-set of looking for something worthy of our attention, inwardly leaning into life with a readiness for noticing when two objects or elements might intersect in an interesting way, motivating either a story or a snapshot. Even without a writing utensil or camera, engaging in observation and curiosity helps us remember that we can still carry this type of perspective into our day. They remind us that our life and the world around us are always speaking to us—all we have to do is choose to listen.

Practice

- What is your life telling you about who you are? Reflect on this day or this past week.

- Next, consider the question from the perspective of your whole life. What have you learned about yourself?

- Notice if you have any fears about *really* listening to what your life is telling you. If so, what are you afraid you might hear?

- Try moving into the day with a sense of curiosity, either thinking of the phrase *Hmm . . . isn't that interesting?* or looking for moments that contain messages worth listening to.

- Consider that what's around you, whether in nature or otherwise, may hold some teachings that are worth paying attention to.

RECLAIMING WHAT'S BEEN LOST

. . . This is what you have been waiting for, he used to say to me. And I'd say, What? And he'd say, This— holding up my cheese and mustard sandwich. And I'd say, What? And he'd say, This, sort of looking around.

— **MARIE HOWE**

Sometimes, what keeps us from fully showing up and listening—what keeps us from seeing that what's in front of us is what we've been waiting for—is that we've become disconnected from some essential aspect of who we are. The wisdom of indigenous cultures speaks to the importance of reclaiming lost qualities that we need in order to fully inhabit our lives. In her work, cultural anthropologist Angeles Arrien describes that in Shamanic societies four questions were presented to someone who complained of emotional or physical dis-ease:

When did you stop singing?
When did you stop dancing?
When did you lose your sense of enchantment with stories, and in particular, your own life story?
When did you become uncomfortable with silence?[4]

These four questions encompass activities that open us up to fully engage with life. And when we lose our connections to these activities, we find we are missing an essential element of our potential.

A dear friend of mine painted a beautiful image based on these four questions. It depicts a vibrant woman whose body is like a fluid tree. In each of the four corners is a symbol associated with song, dance, story, and silence, and it's clear that her body is rooted into each of these aspects of life, offering vitality and joy.

When I look at this picture, I imagine the symbols from the four corners leaping off the page, joining in a circle of people gathered around a fire in ancient times— the kind of gathering that could only occur when there'd been some opportunity to step out of life, to put aside to-do lists and responsibilities, and to strip ourselves of our everyday ways of naming who we are. I imagine these questions being read when there is space and time to sit honestly with the layers of responses that might emerge. How much more might be revealed through this exploration than from our responses to many of the lengthy questionnaires found in most waiting rooms?

When did we stop singing? I love this question, whether we interpret it literally or symbolically. When did we stop letting ourselves fully share with the world what we have to offer and believe that we could make a difference? When did we stop trusting our ability to voice what is true for us?

For many people, this capacity gets shut down in their younger years by the criticism of a parent or teacher. For Ray, it was when he didn't get accepted into a desirable MFA program for creative writing. "I felt so crushed that I never wanted to write again."

It's all too easy to feel that we must be considered talented according to some external set of criteria in order to justify our artistic pursuits. This isn't true when children are younger and are encouraged to sing and paint and sculpt clay objects to their hearts' desire. There often comes a time, however, when people only feel supported in doing these activities if they're going to lead to something. It's not enough to participate in them merely for the sake of enjoyment.

Part of what Ray realized was that his decision not to write was shutting down his sense of creativity. He recognized that his motivation to pursue a degree in writing was mostly out of his desire to have this form of expression be central in his life. To feel more balanced, he realized that he needed to find ways of reconnecting with his love for writing. For starters, he decided to join a local writing group and to attend a workshop in a nearby city.

In Laura's case, she found herself unable to express her opinions when speaking with other parents or fellow volunteers. We looked back to when she had lost this ability because she could remember that as a young child she had been quite outgoing and confident. Sadly, she realized that it was when she had been raped as a teenager. After experiencing this trauma, she no longer felt comfortable speaking her truth. "Gosh, I can see what happened now that I look back. I didn't know how to tell other people what I had gone through, so I figured it was better not to speak up at all. It just seemed safer not to talk."

Gaining this understanding allowed Laura to revisit her beliefs about how to keep herself safe. She knew that she still needed time to heal but realized this could happen without holding back her opinions. In fact, she came to see that speaking her truth was what she most needed to do in order to move beyond her trauma.

In my own life, there was one time that I literally lost my voice over my fear of speaking. I was teaching bedside manner and alternative medicine in a medical school residency program at the time. A faculty member had written a grant to bring this content into their curriculum; however, the subject matter wasn't particularly welcomed by the students or the other faculty members. To make matters worse, unannounced to the physicians, video cameras were installed in all the patient rooms so that they could be videotaped. I was then asked to review these tapes with them.

Soon after this announcement, I walked into the second half of a large meeting. As I entered the room, the chief resident turned to me and said, "Well, speak of the devil. Dr. Horneffer, we were just talking about you." As I sensed the level of frustration and fear among these doctors, beads of sweat formed on my forehead. I could later see how I had become the recipient of a whole host of tensions plaguing the medical education system. Right then, however, I couldn't even think because I was consumed with a queasy, awful feeling—as though I were about to be lynched or tried as a witch.

Not surprisingly, the next day I woke up with laryngitis. Clearly something inside me that was either personal or collective, in current time or from history, didn't feel like it was safe for me to sing, speak, or even whisper. The road back to regaining my voice involved an exploration of how these fears lived inside me and what type of support might come from others around me so I didn't have to feel like I was carrying a lone torch. I also had to reconnect with my passion for the importance of communication skills in health care and for whole-person approaches to healing. The process taught me that to use my voice effectively I had to experience some sense of community—at least so I could feel reasonably safe and supported.

The second question presented is equally powerful: When did we stop dancing? When did we stop our bodies from freely moving, and when did we last allow ourselves to get swept away with the current of life?

Several years ago, when I was teaching a class to adult graduate students, I put on various types of dance music and encouraged everyone to move. At first, they were all quite shy as a group, but as the sounds of drums kept speeding up and they realized that no one was really judging or even looking at them they all started to move and dance, to swing their arms and spin in circles, to skip around the room and at times partner up, mirroring the hand motions of others. It was great fun, and I was struck by how many people commented, "I haven't done that in decades! It never occurred to me that I could put on music and dance around my kitchen!" Something had been liberated that day.

Yoga and tai chi can serve as similar doorways, bringing people back in touch with their bodies and reconnecting them with the joy of movement. In their own ways, both traditions offer a radically different means of relating with ourselves, compared to what most of us are used to. I've called the yoga sessions I offer *juicy yoga,* in part to highlight that in this form of yoga the movement comes from the inside out, beginning with an awareness of what's going on inside of our bodies. With such presence and attention, it's possible for our vitality to radiate out from the center of our being. Throughout the practice, I encourage participants to focus on *how* they're doing what they're doing, more so than on *what* they're doing. Are they present with their breath? Are they noticing how the pose is opening different parts of their body? Are their thoughts focused on what's happening now? Are they being kind with themselves as they move through the sequence of postures?

In order to answer yes to these questions, we have to stay in constant relationship with ourselves. We have to watch the instructor do each pose and then decide if doing that movement is consistent with our body's needs or if we should modify the pose to better support ourselves. From this perspective, I'm always thrilled to look out and see no two people doing the same thing as they make their practices their own. It also makes me smile to know that this form of exercise allows them to relate to their bodies very differently than how they might when looking at their reflection in the mirror.

As we gain a greater ability to be present in our bodies, we can also gain a greater ability to more fully embody the story of who we are. We need to connect to the story of our own life—coming to see that we have a story to share and to build on. A friend told me how her son had written a poem for her birthday titled "She Who Loves to Walk with Cats." I commented how cool it was that he really saw who she was: an animal lover, a person who enjoys moving through nature in day-to-day life. We noted how, in some Native American traditions, this could have been the name given to her. The conversation made me reflect on how others might name themselves: "She who loves to . . . " "He who is a lover of this or that . . . " It made me think about how writing this type of sentence might reconnect us to what our life holds, what seeds we want to water, and how we want our stories to unfold.

Viewing our life as a story is powerful because it highlights our role in creating what's to come. It reminds us that we don't have to stay trapped in the story line of our past, given that narratives have the potential to shift and surprise us in all sorts of ways. In Laura's journey of reclaiming her ability to speak, it was essential for her to consciously bring the trauma she experienced into the story of her life. We worked together to find ways in which she could do this without allowing the experience of being raped to become the sole occurrence that defined her life or the final sentence in naming who she was. It helped her to keep coming back to the question, "And now what?" as a way of exploring how her past wanted to *inform* her future without preventing her from *fully inhabiting* her future.

Often, a key to reclaiming our story is having the capacity and the opportunity to be silent. I've encountered many people who, when asked when they lost their comfort with silence, respond by saying, "I don't think I ever was comfortable being quiet." With a little encouragement, we can gain comfort with silence and, often, what we come to see is that the qualities we're most at risk of losing are those things that can only be known by contacting the silent places within ourselves. The best things in life often border on being intangible or at least fluid in their nature—relationships, love, unexpected moments of feeling grateful for the sandwich that sits right in front of us. Because of their lack of density, they can easily escape our attention without periodic encounters with silence and the reflection that this allows.

Practice

- Take some time to reflect on these four questions. Reword them as needed so that they make sense within the context of your life:

    ◆ When did you stop singing?

    ◆ When did you stop dancing?

    ◆ When did you lose your sense of enchantment with stories, and in particular, your own life story?

- When did you become uncomfortable with silence?

- Are there any other aspects of who you are and what your life is about that have gotten lost along the way? What might you do to reclaim these qualities?

In order to fully inhabit our days, it's important that we find our own versions of butter to embrace, our own ways of noticing and listening to the world around us, and our own strategies for reclaiming the aspects of ourselves that can get lost along the way. By encouraging ourselves to pay attention in these ways, we can continue bringing the best of our inner wisdom to our outer life, and we can allow our outer life to contribute to the richness of our inner journey as well.

REMEMBERING LIGHTNESS

*. . . Nearby is the country they call life. You will know it
by its seriousness. Give me your hand.*

—RILKE

I was going through airport security the other
month, participating in the grind of pulling out my
laptop and my Ziploc baggie full of plastic bottles—and
removing my belt and my shoes and my watch and
my jacket and trying to fit them all into the plastic bin
in such a way that nothing would fall out as it went
through its screening.

On the other side, I quickly gathered my belongings
so that they wouldn't get run over by the oncoming
stream of objects. I started shuffling forward with my
shoes half on and my arms weighed down by my scat-
tering of possessions. As I glanced up, I saw a group of
chairs and tables with an accompanying sign that read:
"Recombobulation Area."

"Ha!" I grunted with laughter and relief. "How perfect is that!"

Not only did I appreciate having some space to pull
myself together, but even more so, I loved that someone
had invented this word and had gone to the effort of
naming this area—I loved how it created a moment of

unexpected lightness, especially when I was feeling a bit bogged down.

I'm not quite sure why the human maturation process so often involves a movement away from such humor and lightness and toward the more serious aspects of life. Why is it that studies show that adults laugh far fewer times a day than children? I do understand the need to become responsible as we enter adulthood; unfortunately, this responsibility often seems to get paired with the wilting of some essential part of us.

On the one hand, the arrival of heaviness makes sense. Life is serious, and its seriousness becomes more apparent as we grow up and come to see life for what it is and what it isn't. We can feel life narrowing as our world no longer contains infinite possibilities but rather a defined reality with deadlines and bills and other responsibilities. Things feel less shiny and new, and, on top of this, life becomes more serious when serious things happen like illnesses or the loss of relationships, loved ones, or jobs.

Even in our efforts to better ourselves and carve out worthy and meaningful lives, we can become tense and rigid in our pursuits because of the importance they hold. In naming the ingredients that are supposed to add up to a successful life, lightness is often forgotten. Maybe it's just that the sheer busyness of adulthood causes us to forget. After years of counseling, I've seen that this piece is often missing in marriages and partnerships that are strained and in people who are struggling. As to-do lists increase and the balance between work and home gets more complicated, humor and fun depart. We can forget that there's value in loosening our reins, putting down our lists, and being willing to laugh at ourselves when life humbles us. Without these gestures, we lose a key buffer that protects our souls from the demands of the world.

I can recall going to a counseling session when I was a graduate student. In a serious and somber way, I described some of the pressures I was feeling in my program and my reasons for coming for counseling. As I waited for my therapist to offer a formal assessment of the situation, she responded, "Well, from what I'm hearing, that sounds really fucked up."

Her words made me laugh, and along with validating my experience, they also lightened my perspective. It was a moment that reminded me that humor creates a sense of space, where otherwise there is none.

Every day, I see the power of creating this sense of space in my work as a therapist. It's not that my agenda is to be funny or to make people laugh when they are in agony, but the truth is that often part of what contributes to our suffering is being disconnected from any sense of lightness—and thus disconnected from our capacity for acceptance and gratitude as well. In some moments, being surprised by a colorful metaphor or a playful comparison can knock us out of our entrenched point of view so that we can see life in a new way.

One of my favorite incidents of lightness changing my perspective came after I had driven across the country to move into my brand-new apartment. I had painfully written out my deposit check months beforehand for an amount that approximated my monthly student income. When I arrived, I was horrified to find millipedes covering the floor. They were moving around everywhere, with some curled up in tiny balls. All I wanted to do in response was curl up myself. I called a friend to share my woes and had a strange exchange of words.

"You're kidding me?" she said. "There are that many? How did they get in, and what on earth are they doing there?"

"I don't know how they got in," I said, "but they seem pretty content to just lie around all over the floor."

"Why aren't they on the furniture?"

"Because the moving van hasn't come yet."

"Well, have you tried to talk with them, to ask them why they are there?"

"What?" I exclaimed.

"The people from the Philippines. Have you asked them why they are there?"

In this moment, I started to laugh so hard that I didn't even mind the infestation in my apartment. It was such a ridiculous conversation that it changed my whole mood and perspective.

This is the magic of humor. It can make life bearable in moments that would otherwise be unbearable. It helps keep marriages, partnerships, and careers sustainable. When we can adopt this lens of humor, we can be much more creative in our responses to life.

Rich and Lorin came to see me because they had been noticing how the tension between them had heightened since the birth of their third child nine months before. As Lorin explained, "It's just that we're so stretched between the three kids. I think we're permanently pissed at each other—maybe for no other reason than that there's so much to do, and it feels like the other person should always be doing more."

"One thing's for certain," Rich added. "Any humor that ever was in our home has gone out the window."

We talked about better ways in which they could divide up some of the tasks of parenting, but more important, we discussed how the two of them could find their way back to being on the same team. They came to see that when they were most needing each other and needing to work together they were, instead, using each other as a target for their stress. I asked them what it would be like to surrender to the reality that for the next months it might feel like there's always more to do than time to do it in—and to see that this wasn't anyone's fault. Would it be possible to draw on humor as a way to come together in the impossibility of their predicament?

To offer a lighter note, I retold a story that had arrived in my e-mail the week before. It described an old man who was grocery shopping with his grandson—a toddler who kept crying and at times screaming at the top of his lungs. As the old gentleman walked up and down the aisles, people could hear him speaking in a soft voice . . . "We are almost done, Albert . . . Try not to cry, Albert . . . Life will get better, Albert . . . "

As the man was paying the cashier, a young woman in line behind him said, "Sir, I think it is wonderful how sweet you are being to your little Albert," to which the gentleman replied, "Miss, my grandson's name is John . . . I'm Albert."

In the same spirit of Albert, I encouraged Rich and Lorin to consider playfully reminding each other, in trying moments, that their current circumstances were temporary—*"Try not to cry. . . Life will get better. . . "*

We also identified several ways they could bring some lightness back into their home. They asked their older son and daughter to find some good joke books at the library and to share one or two at night before going to bed. Rich and Lorin also talked about how he, in particular, used to be quite playful and silly, imitating cartoon characters with perfect intonation. Possibly he could bring some of this back into their mealtimes, along with some playfulness in having themed dinners around certain food colors and shapes. They liked how these ideas would also invite their older children to participate—lightening the mood for everyone.

Tom, another person I work with, didn't need to find lightness in his parenting, but he was in need of finding ways to deal with the stress of his workplace. His company was in the middle of a merger, and he was a key player in the negotiations. He found himself so wrapped up in the stress of the situation that he had hardly smiled in a month. "It doesn't help that I haven't gotten to do any of my hobbies since this negotiation started."

Week after week, he'd come to my office, updating me on the latest saga. One day he commented, "This negotiation is so crazy, you'd think it was out of a movie."

Knowing that he played around with animation, I suggested, "Maybe you should make a movie about it."

At first he laughed at the idea, but then a smile came over his face as he began to dream up how he could make simple clay figures for each of his co-workers. He realized that this type of creative process might offer him a way to gain some distance and perspective on the whole situation.

He decided to film an *episode* every week to reflect the ongoing drama. "I think my co-workers are a bit puzzled when I don't get rattled in the way I used to. Little do they know that in those moments I'm imaging how my clay figures will have to be reshaped and moved around to reflect the latest development."

For Becky, she needed to lighten up around her wellness efforts. While she knew it was a good idea to commit to losing the 20 pounds she had gained, she found herself being agitated and stressed to a degree that didn't feel healthy. "Actually, it was my partner, Marcy, who pointed out that ever since I've gone on this diet I've been no fun to be around. I guess I can see her point—but I'm trying to take this seriously, and there's a lot involved between weighing certain foods and counting calories and having to avoid half the foods she loves to eat."

Becky and I talked about how she might invite Marcy to support her in losing weight, maybe by calling on her cooking skills to help make some of the low-fat dishes more interesting. Marcy decided to have some fun with this by making Becky guess what spices she had added and then coming up with different low-calorie desserts on the weekends. They also worked together to come up with a reward system for Becky's efforts. To add some levity, they decided to create a sticker chart on the refrigerator with prizes that could be earned each week. Becky also decided to ask several friends if they could e-mail her some encouraging and humorous quotes to support her in keeping a positive attitude as she worked toward her goal.

The beauty of using humor and keeping a sense of lightness and playfulness in our life is that it helps us deal with life as it is—the ups and downs, the unexpected changes, and the frustrations we may encounter.

A great example of the buffer allowed by lightness came on a day when my husband had been traveling and I had arranged for a sitter in order to have several hours of some much-needed alone time—I was hoping to bring my attention inward, in the spirit of taking the best of my own advice to turn within. I felt giddy as she arrived, and I quickly oriented her to what she could serve my children for dinner and told her about a few new games they might want to play together. I scurried upstairs to my bedroom, where I had already laid out several poetry books, my journal, and a favorite pen. I fluffed up my buckwheat-filled meditation cushion and lit a candle.

"Ahhh," I sighed.

I began my time by reading a passage from Rilke: "Go into yourself and see how deep the place is from which your life flows."[1]

I sat for several minutes, quieting the thoughts in my mind and allowing the invitation of Rilke's words to sink into my awareness. I started to notice the rhythm of my breathing, and I felt a sense of calm arrive.

"Ahhh," I sighed again.

I felt inspired to draw an image in my journal, and so I went to get some colored pencils from my office down the hallway. As I opened my bedroom door, I heard the words, "Well, maybe we should go get Mom and tell her." And then I heard the sitter say, "No, I think it's okay."

Bless her, I thought, and I fought the impulse to go downstairs.

Don't you dare, I said to myself. *This is your time to be with Rilke and the place from which your life flows.*

I got my colored pencils and walked back to my bedroom with resolve. As I closed the door I heard the sitter say, "Don't worry, honey. I don't think any of the eggs have hatched yet . . . "

I sat down on my cushion, determined to stay calm and present with my journal and candle and breath. It was hard, however, not to feel haunted by her words.

Eggs? I thought. *I made macaroni and cheese for dinner. Why is she talking about eggs?*

My mind kept scanning its inner reference points to eggs, much as I tried to keep my attention on my breath. Soon, I was consumed with my puzzling to the point where I felt my forehead squint into a crease.

"Oh shit!" I said out loud as I remembered noticing my son's dry scalp that morning—how I had encouraged him to use some dandruff shampoo to see if it would help.

I blew out my candle flame and closed my journal, letting out much more of a moan than a sigh this time.

Needless to say, the last thing in the world I wanted to do was blow out that flame. I didn't want to drive out to the drugstore, or to have conversations about lice, or to comb hair under bright lights. I wanted my time alone.

It helped me find some lightness in the situation when I started to wonder, *Did Rilke ever have to deal with a case of head lice in his family? And how about the other contemplative saints throughout history? How about Thoreau on Walden Pond? I bet he never had to deal with such a thing.* Somehow, letting my mind entertain these thoughts helped to make a disappointing situation a little less disappointing. It also helped me to appreciate what the evening did offer, which ended up being many sweet and amusing moments with my children.

When we bring a humorous lens to moments like this, not only does it make them more bearable, but it can also allow us to recognize that these types of disappointments and derailings of our spiritual practice are actually valuable spiritual practices in and of themselves. With a little lightness and humor, we're able to see our attachments, just as we would in a meditation practice—and we also end up developing greater levels of flexibility, just as we might from attending a yoga class. Such moments highlight how choosing a lens of humor can be a valuable spiritual practice.

Practice

- Where in your life could you use some humor and lightness: in your relationships, at work, in your ways of approaching self-care?

- What are some ways of lightening up your life that would work for you?

- What might be the benefits of such lightness for you—possibly feeling less stressed or finding a greater sense of acceptance or creativity or gratitude in life?

- Are there stressful situations you can reframe, possibly imagining them to be part of the plot in line in a comedy? (Of course, you don't have to make clay figures.) Play with this mind-set during the week as life challenges you or seems utterly serious. See if this helps to shift your felt sense of busyness.

FINDING ENCHANTMENT

Don't ask yourself what the world needs. Ask yourself what makes you come alive and then do it. Because what the world needs is people who have come alive.

— HOWARD THURMAN

The average adult who goes to Disney World will walk away with two primary responses. First, they'll note that what Disney sets out to do it does very well; and second, they'll realize that they've just spent a lot of money to create the very same experiences that on any other day they'd try to avoid (like spending a lot of money). This realization came to me several years ago, when I was waiting in long lines amid congested crowds of people in the hot sun in my quest to ride down a fake river in a contrived raft. Over the course of four days, not only did I make it down the river, but I was also thrown, spun, flung, dropped, scared, and repeatedly knocked over by an enormous wave. I basically paid to have the shit kicked out of me in the name of being entertained.

And interestingly, I was. As I gripped my bathing suit top for dear life while being engulfed by a typhoon, I felt utterly alive. The people around me seemed alive as well. It was a contrast to the experience of walking down a city street and seeing solemn and distant faces. Here everyone was present. They were animated and vocal, gasping every time the wave would start to come and recounting their adventures to those standing near them as the wave passed. There seemed to be a simplicity in their joy that resembled an infant dropping an object off his high chair over and over and being delighted by its magical return.

As I walked around Mickey's kingdom, I wondered why our average towns can't feel this magical. Isn't that really what we want—to feel this quality of enchantment and lightness in day-to-day life?

I see a yearning for this in how trees stretch up toward the sun, how we look forward to vacations, even in how children draw people's hands as large open circles with fingers radiating outward. I see it in the actions of my great-aunt, who in her mid-90s hitchhiked to see Engelbert Humperdinck in concert. It's all the same impulse. We want to feel good, to feel happy, to feel alive. Maybe, too, along with wanting to show up fully in life and see the beauty around us we also want to be knocked over and swept away from time to time—to fall in love with life and feel enchanted by what it has to offer.

Finding our way to this type of aliveness and enchantment isn't always a simple task. One obstacle is that, as a culture, we seem to have a hard time figuring out how to be in relationships with good things. In some ways, our society ignores them. We only have to watch the news to see that happy topics are rarely newsworthy. Leaning in the other direction, our culture, at times, has oversimplified how to feel good. For example, the encouragement in the 1980s to *just think positive* suggested that by chopping off our darkness and *willing* ourselves toward happiness and aliveness we would find our way there. Maybe as a response to such suggestions, people became a bit suspicious about being positive: questioning if people who are happy are also shallow, or selfish, or even up to something illegal.

The journey toward aliveness is also complicated, because what ignites each of us differs. We don't all want to go to an amusement park. Even parts of me didn't want to go to Disney World, feeling much more content to sit in a cabin by the woods. I'm reminded of the movie *Pleasantville,* in which each of the characters comes into full color at a particular point. For one, it's when she decides to take care of her own needs. For another, it's when he finally honors his true passion in life. My favorite, however, is an adolescent boy who stands up for someone else by slugging a bully. In the moment of stepping into his courage, he comes more fully alive.

I love theologian Howard Thurman's encouragement that we need to explore what makes us come alive—that sitting with this question is more an obligation than a luxury. Sometimes we need to consider this question in terms of what can bring enjoyment and excitement to our lives. Sometimes, too, the key to our aliveness lies in the intersection between what we love to do and how this activity might meet the greater needs of our local or global community. There's nothing like making a difference in the world around us to offer a sense of meaning and fulfillment in our lives.

I've also seen that as we explore what enlivens us and offers us a sense of enchantment we need to consider what withers us as well. In workshops, I have people reflect on this question by first drawing a large ying-yang circle, with one side representing *things that make you come alive* and the other side representing *things that deplete you*. I encourage people to really think about what they write on each side, not assuming that activities that are stereotypically thought of as being enjoyable or exhausting necessarily show up that way for them.

Rachael commented that she was surprised to realize that the book club she'd been in for five years didn't really enliven her to nearly the degree she had assumed. "I started to write it down on the 'enlivening' side of the drawing, but then I had to be honest with myself about how many times I haven't really liked the book selection and have needed to rush to finish it. It's making me think that maybe I'd rather use that time to volunteer at our school library."

Carol chimed in that she was surprised to realize how little she enjoyed going out to big parties. "As I sat with this drawing I realized that ten years ago I would have written 'parties' in huge letters to reflect how much I loved being social, but probably a party a month is plenty for me at this point in my life. What nourishes me more than anything after a long week is to rent a movie and curl up with a blanket and a bucket of popcorn."

While Nancy was filling in her drawing, she recognized something about her time at home. "It hadn't occurred to me that although I complain about all the housework I'm stuck with when my kids leave for school and my husband heads off to work, I actually love being alone in my house. It's very restorative. I can put on folk music without complaints from anyone and simply be with my own thoughts, uninterrupted. I guess I haven't recognized how valuable this time is for me."

I know for myself, when I think about what provides a sense of aliveness for me, one thing that comes to mind is new experiences. I always feel inspired by hearing about people's new interests or hobbies, as well as learning about different ways that people spice up their days that I've never thought of before. Just like humor, experiencing new sights and other ways of living can help shift our perspective.

When I was visiting Bali, I happened upon some Westerners who had relocated permanently and were discussing a problem they were currently facing. Their concerns opened my eyes to an issue I knew nothing about—and it certainly made me see life in a more colorful way.

"I think it's time to get my monkey a hysterectomy," said the woman sitting across from me on a velour sofa. It was when I heard this that I turned to face her, curious to hear more.

"Yes," she continued, shaking her head, "I was so hoping it wouldn't come to this, but the scratch marks on my arm are healing so slowly. It keeps getting worse every month."

"What?" I chimed in, having no way to fill in the missing pieces of what she was saying as I so often do when overhearing half of a conversation.

"Ginger, my monkey . . . Did you see her next door as you walked up? She has the beautiful blue eyelids that look like she's applied eye shadow. Oh, she's a doll, but she's always liked Henry more than me, and her jealousy is getting ridiculous. Is it right that I get attacked for walking into my own home and coming over to greet my husband?"

"Well, no . . . " I started to say.

"And I can't bear the thought of getting rid of her, so the doctor suggested maybe we try a full hysterectomy to curb her attraction to Henry."

I nodded in hopes of seeming empathic, as my friend chimed in, "Monkeys sure can be rascals." He was spinning a glass in his hand, attempting to break apart the ice cubes that had clumped together. "I still remember my pet monkey when I was a kid. Charles was his name. One day, my mom was having a party with some country club friends, and Charles ran right up one of the women's skirts. Boy, was that a hoot!"

"You had a pet monkey in Michigan?" I interrupted.

"Oh yeah—we would take baths together and then dry him with our blow-dryer until his hair was standing straight up!"

I felt a tap on my shoulder by Ginger's owner, who had moved closer to me. "Monkeys don't like to be wet or cold," she whispered, and then leaned back, seeming confident that this detail had helped the whole conversation make sense.

I looked around the room, thinking I must have missed out on taking the drugs that these people had taken. I expected to spot some lines of a powdery substance, or at least an ashtray or a deep-colored beverage. But all I could find were innocent glasses of lemonade and iced tea.

Ginger's owner tapped me on the shoulder again and asked, "Have you traveled much?"

"No, not really," I replied, sensing that she probably already knew the answer to her question. "But now that the kids are a little older we're hoping to take more trips."

In hearing this, her friend lit up. "Oh, there are so many places to see: the Galápagos Islands are amazing, New Zealand—"

"That reminds me of our trip to Australia," Ginger's owner interrupted. "Do you remember that man who owned the shark-seeing business? He had created a cage to take people down into the ocean, right up close to the sharks. I'll never forget the sight of him standing, with only one arm, in front of a sign that read: 'New and Improved Cage.' And people still came!"

It was around this point that I fully registered how far I was from home. My laughter poured out, not only at the image of the one-armed shark man but also at the cumulative crescendo of tales. These people's zest for life was contagious, and I found myself feeling more alive, as though I had shared in their adventures.

I realize that such moments can't happen all the time and that what sometimes makes us feel light will at other times weigh us down. If I had to travel and experience new things constantly, I imagine I would feel the fatigue of my adventures. And the same goes for our everyday lives—those activities that enliven us when done intermittently end up depleting us when done for long stretches of time.

Cheryl recognized that by the end of her weekly *catch-up day* she always felt exhausted. "I always start by making a list of my chores to do, bills to pay, phone calls to make, and computer tasks to complete. The problem is that by the time I do any one of these tasks, I feel drained—either by how physically demanding it is to clean the floors and dust the house, or by how much my shoulders ache after slumping over my computer for hours. It's a different type of exhaustion that comes from talking to people on the phone." Although Cheryl's intentions for having a catch-up day were right on target, she needed to alternate the types of activities she was doing as opposed to creating a marathon out of each set of tasks.

A month later she came back and was thrilled at the difference this shift had made. "I have so much more energy at the end of the day if I allow myself to move around with what I'm doing. Either I do two tasks on each list and then switch, or I notice when I'm starting to feel fatigued and move on to something different. It's also helped me to play some music when I'm cleaning, and to allow myself a few ten-minute naps throughout the day to regain my energy."

Cheryl's shift in approaching her to-do list is a great example of how we can enliven activities that tend to be dull or draining. Another common activity that people find withering is waiting. When one adds up the time spent stopped at red lights, stuck in traffic jams, standing in lines, being put on hold, and sitting in waiting rooms it amounts to a sizable number of minutes. It makes it worth considering how we might use this time to have it feel less wasteful and irritating. I've heard people commit to bringing books to read, puzzles to solve, letters to finish, games to play, or to using the time simply to take a few deep breaths.

When Bob heard others naming these examples, he realized that he needed to come up with a strategy for handling long waits at restaurants. "It drives me nuts when I go out to eat and there's poor service or a long wait due to crowds. I almost always end up getting angry at the waitstaff, which leaves my wife threatening to boycott eating out with me. Maybe I should try working on my crossword puzzles, and having her help me, as a way to divert my attention."

Whether it's by helping buffer the draining aspects of our day-to-day life or by adding in a sense of adventure and enchantment in a more spirited way, it's important that we periodically revisit what needs to happen to help us feel fully alive.

Practice

- Consider doing the ying-yang exercise described. Create one side that depicts *things that make you come alive* and the other representing *things that deplete you.* Be honest with yourself about what shows up in both sections. Is there anything that surprises you?

- How can you shift the timing of when or how you do certain activities to lessen the ways in which they exhaust you?

- Are there ways you can enliven the potentially mundane tasks of everyday life, like waiting?

- How might you spice up your life with some new adventuresome activities? What would be your version of getting a pet monkey?

Coming Up Fresh

We live our lives, do whatever we do, and then we sleep—
it's as simple and ordinary as that . . . There's just this for
consolation: an hour here or there when our lives seem,
against all odds and expectations, to burst open and
give us everything we've ever imagined . . .

— M ICHAEL C UNNINGHAM

Living a life filled with passion and playfulness is one of the most powerful ways of bringing lightness into our lives. I sit with many people who feel disconnected from a sense of passion and who feel disenchanted by what adult life has been distilled into. There's almost a shrinking quality as they describe the ways in which key relationships feel wilted and as they name the consequences of what's lost as so many hours are poured into the responsibilities that accompany all the things they so desired acquiring: families, homes, respectable jobs. It's as though the box of crayons they once held in life has shrunk to a much smaller size.

In contrast, there are other people I can think of who have found ways not only to hold on to their crayons but also to add new colors as they make the passage through adulthood. I think of those who have pursued second careers or who have started nonprofit organizations in order to follow their passion, those who have returned to their love of painting with watercolors or learned to play musical instruments at a later age. I'm also reminded of my high school math teacher who was so excited about calculus that even after 25 years of teaching he drew us to the edges of our seats as he would lecture. I don't know that I ever fully grasped the concepts he was presenting, but I did come to know from watching the sparkle in his eye that the beauty of numbers kept his soul alive.

Maybe it matters less where we find passion in our lives. What's more important is simply that we continue to find sources of amusement and inspiration so that we don't lose our capacity to be delighted or to delight others.

At times, either in small ways or not so small ways, we may feel ourselves getting constricted in how we've come to define our life story, as if we're wearing a shoe that's too tight for us. I can think of a simple example of this when I was in college, shopping with a friend. I was drawn to a certain long sweater with large buttons and a colorful print. As I pulled it from the rack to try on, my friend commented, "You know that sweater doesn't look anything like you." She was probably accurate with her comment, but it struck me that if I purchased the sweater and started wearing it a lot it would look like me or, more accurately, I would look like it—maybe something in me was wanting to become a bit more colorful.

Examples like this demonstrate how, even in subtle ways, we can find ourselves being molded into some way of being, simply out of habit, and out of wanting to be consistent and predictable for others in our lives. Of course, it's not that we're always conscious of the ways we might feel pressured to stay the same—nor would we want to become different only to be different or to make changes that feel inauthentic. Given, though, that the winds of life naturally create change within us, it's important that we stay in conversation with who we're becoming and who we want to be.

As Linda reflected on this idea of being in conversation with herself, she realized that she needed to leave her dating relationship. "He makes me feel guilty for wanting to get back into ice-skating and for taking cooking classes. All he wants to do on the weekends is stay home and rent movies, and I want to get out and see some local theater and live music. I was sharing my New Year's resolution around learning a new language, and maybe even opening a food pantry on our side of town. He just thinks I'm crazy."

In Linda's case, she realized that in order to bring lightness into her life she needed to redefine some part of her way of being. For her, some of these new activities were about returning to a quality of playfulness that she had when she was younger.

In my case, that desire to reconnect with playfulness came through having children. It was early on in my pregnancy that my husband began to joke with me, questioning if this was my primary motivation for bearing offspring. "Parenting is not just about coming up with Halloween costumes and throwing birthday parties for your own sake," he had reminded me repeatedly, part in jest and part in seriousness.

I think his first warnings were a foreshadowing of events to come: having my one-year-old son dress as a parrot in order to accessorize my pirate costume, renting an inflatable moonwalk as a birthday party surprise. As I attempted to explain, "I would have told you, but sometimes it's hard to see that something's a good idea until it's fully inflated and sitting on your front lawn."

I've heard other parents make similar confessions. As Sharon noted, "It's nice to have an excuse to see cartoon movies, and I have to say, I've enjoyed spending time playing on the floor and getting time outside when we go to parks." I can recall attending toddler music classes and laughing with the other mothers about how we all came as much for ourselves as for our kids. For me, I know it was a stress relief: seeing other kids misbehaving more than mine and, better yet, playing a triangle, and a drum, and that thing that you roll between your hands to make the two wooden balls swing back and forth.

I realize there were moments that I got a little carried away. At story time in the first class, I found myself blurting out answers with the toddlers—or, even worse, just before them.

"What does a cow say?"

I know! I know! I'd think, and soon a large and loud, "Mooo," would be passing through my lips before I could censor it.

But hanging out with children is only one portal into the playfulness and aliveness of our youth. Listening to music from our younger years is another wonderful way to dust off this part of ourselves. I discovered this the first night I brought home a new minivan and was introduced to the '70s and '80s channels on the satellite radio. I went out to run a quick errand and found myself reconnecting with songs from my past that I had forgotten all about. It was like attending a high school reunion, remeeting classmates and recalling lost memories, and then attending a middle school reunion and a summer camp reunion. It was a reunion with the best of parties and the thrill of making out in a car, the vulnerability of school dances, and the freedom of performing to invisible audiences in my bedroom.

The problems didn't begin until the next day, when I was driving my kids home from school. This was when I found myself singing along enthusiastically without thinking about the implications. It wasn't that the lyrics to the song were really that bad. What was problematic was more the emotional outpouring that followed.

"I used to love these guys! They wore these inverted red flowerpots on their heads and silver metallic one-piece space suits that you could buy from an order form in their record album. They were so cool!" As I was continuing to sing and shimmy my head back and forth, my eyes happened to glance in the rearview mirror and catch the expression on my son's face. It was a cross between horror and disbelief, like somehow his mother was an alien born from these men in their metallic space suits. From the look on his face, I feared that everything I had ever said or taught, any rule or guideline I had created for our family, was now null and void by virtue of the fact that I had ever patronized these musicians— had ever bought albums, memorized lyrics, or nagged my parents for money to purchase the flowerpot hat.

I tried to defend myself, but I could tell my explanations were pointless. Instead, it was becoming more apparent that my children watching me reconnect with my childhood wasn't nearly as tidy or impressive as when I merely *talked* about my childhood by pulling up select stories for teaching moments or justification of parenting responses.

"I used to have to eat *all* of my vegetables."

"I saw a total of four movies as a kid, and there weren't even video stores back then."

As I realized the mounting danger at hand, I decided, at least for a while, to change my pre-set channels before more damage could be done. I've learned that it's better to wait until my kids aren't in the car to travel back in time.

But that doesn't detract from how refreshing and revitalizing it can be to reconnect with these sorts of memories from our youth. Such escapes can help offset how we often get the short end of the stick in day-to-day life, as adults. Not only do we have to deal with finances and other responsibilities, but we no longer have people making efforts to amuse and entertain us by handing us crayons, tucking prizes in our cereal boxes, or including bright designs on our backpacks and plates.

Just to be fair, I must admit that there came a day, about two years ago, when I was offered a perk as an adult. I was riding in the business section of a ferry, and as I was enjoying the quiet joys of traveling alone a woman appeared with a tray piled high with baked goods.

"Chocolate-covered macaroon, ma'am?" she asked with a smile. "They're complimentary to our business-class guests."

"You're kidding me?" I said. "Really? For me? Gosh yes, I'll take one." I was thrilled, even though I don't even really care for macaroons.

While we are sometimes offered such nuggets of joy, the thing we need to learn as adults is that, in a sense, adulthood is much like late February during a cold winter, when the novelty of snow has worn off and people have to dig a little deeper for their joy. I often think of this when I hear adults describing the things that make their days feel fresh and joyful: knitting, gardening, singing in choirs, downhill skiing, learning to surf, barefoot running, ballroom dancing, volunteering, gourmet cooking, going to concerts, riding horses, training dogs, mountain climbing, reading novels—the list goes on and on.

As adults, we have to take responsibility for finding and refinding our own versions of fun, engaging in whatever activities allow us to reconnect with a sense of excitement and freedom and goodness—and maybe the best of our youth as well.

You may think of yourself as a travel-size box of crayons,
holding only the primary colors.
But I promise you are at least a 64 box, maybe an 86 box
(how large do they come these days?).
And yes, the sharpener is included.

Practice

- Are there aspects of your life that have gotten too narrowly defined?

- What brings you joy, fun, and amusement?

- Are there new activities you'd like to try or activities you used to do that possibly you'd like to dust off and revisit? These may be hobbies that are purely for your entertainment or endeavors that might be both fun as well as of value to those around you.

Bringing lightness to our life is a highly personal endeavor. For some people, embracing humor and laughter, along with high-spirited adventure, is a good fit for their personality. It's what allows their life to come into full color. For others, it may be more subtle ways of lightening up life that feel right—a slight shift in how they relate to their thoughts and feelings, a few simple touches added to their everyday tasks, or the simple joy that comes from bringing lightness to others. When thinking about remembering lightness, it's not necessary that we chuckle out loud or visibly smile. What's more important is that we find our own version of a smile within ourselves.

EMBRACING DIFFICULTY

The main spiritual question is how you relate to difficulty.

— PEMA CHÖDRÖN

For most people, exploring ways to lighten up our days sounds much more appealing than examining how we respond to the inevitable difficulties in life. I've seen, however, that the ways we relate to these two streams of lightness and difficulty are equally essential to our well-being. Not surprisingly, both are intertwined with our experience of busyness in their different ways. While having overly filled days can prevent us from accessing lightness in life, sometimes what's behind our choice to be busy, consciously or unconsciously, is a desire to avoid feeling our pain.

If we can get away without spending time revisiting difficult emotions and memories and allow them to simply move through us, then . . . why not? This is similar to the logic used with relaxation practices. If we can simply exhale, let go, and move into resting, then this is the obvious choice. Sometimes, however, when people feel tense it's better for them to introduce more intentional tightness into their body before attempting to relax. This can be seen in approaches like progressive muscle relaxation, in which participants first are asked to consciously tighten certain muscle groups, holding the squeeze for several breaths and then to release both their self-created tension and the tightness that already existed. Here the release is facilitated by first exaggerating the stress.

The expression *If you can't get out of it, get into it* is saying basically the same thing. When this course of action is needed, we usually know it. We notice our minds circling through their ruminations, the way our breath catches, and maybe a sinking feeling in our gut— all suggesting that something has hooked us. It's understandable that our typical human response is to wish that these feelings would go away. When they don't, however, it's useful to recognize them as opportunities to understand ourselves more deeply. When we imagine them to be a trailhead of sorts, we become open to the possibility that we're being led down a necessary path of self-growth.

I spend a lot of time talking about these crossroad moments, exploring how we tend to respond to them and whether or not we even notice them. It helps to be aware of our typical ways of coping with the arrival of unpleasant emotions, whether it's being in denial, becoming anxious, drinking alcohol, or getting busier. As Margaret confessed, "Now I see that when I feel overwhelmed by life, I blame others. The situation quickly becomes about how my kids didn't pick up their things, how my husband doesn't help out enough, how my colleagues aren't on the ball. Even if I'm not blaming others overtly, I'm thinking critical thoughts about them. I've just never thought about doing it differently."

When Margaret attempted to bring herself into the equation, she saw how she would simply direct her blame and criticism inside. In seeing this, she came to understand why it felt easier to keep her focus outside of herself.

Learning constructive ways of turning our attention within is one of the most useful skills we can acquire. As Buddhist philosophy reminds us, most human suffering can be boiled down to moments of not getting what we want or getting what we don't want. Given the commonality of these experiences, it's useful to learn how to relate to difficulty so we don't continually rely on familiar, habitual coping strategies that may not even work.

For most of us, these strategies are attempts to distract ourselves from simply being present with pain. Over time, the lengths we go to in order to push away difficult feelings often create more pain than if we were to simply *get into it.* In Margaret's case, I encouraged her to consider what it would be like not to blame others and not to blame herself. Would it be possible for her to sit with the emotion of being overwhelmed and to really pay attention to what that experience was like in her body, heart, and mind? I asked her to notice if her experience of being overwhelmed felt more like heaviness or chaos, more like sadness or fear. Often, we don't realize such subtleties; we're so busy attempting to jump out of an experience that we don't allow ourselves to know it. It's a bit like running around yelping about a monster in the closet, rather than opening the closet to see what this perceived monster really is.

In Margaret's situation, it may be that others really are to blame. Possibly her kids and husband and colleagues truly aren't carrying their share of the weight, leaving her to pick up the pieces. Even so, it's still helpful if Margaret can stay with her own inner experiences as opposed to immediately turning her focus on others. Sometimes, too, difficult situations arise where the construct of blame doesn't really fit, highlighting how the act of blaming is mostly an attempt to cope with intense emotion. Buddhist teacher Pema Chödrön demonstrates this in recounting a Zen story about a man who's paddling on a river at dusk. He sees a boat coming toward him. As it approaches, he begins to scream and shake his fist. Only after the boat hits his boat does he realize that it's empty.[1] Sometimes in life we find ourselves, similarly cursing at situations that are empty of blame.

My enthusiasm about embracing unwanted feelings is as much an attempt to convince myself as anyone else. As they say, we teach what we need to learn. I find it helpful to be reminded of the benefits that come from leaning into these dark places, including the idea that this leaning allows us to work with and not against our emotions. When we push away feelings that aren't ready to leave, these feelings can get even larger and messier, as though they're standing up to a bully. In such pushing, we also create emotional tension by forming a polarity in our psyche, with one part of us feeling one way and another part of us not wanting that feeling to exist. Often, this tug-of-war becomes a greater source of distress than the original emotion.

Jim experienced this in relation to his grown son, Mike. He felt heartbroken by the fact that Mike rarely contacted him. He wanted a closer relationship but feared it would never happen because, for years, he had not been involved in Mike's life after his divorce from Mike's mother. At the same time, it drove Jim nuts that he cared so much. "I can't believe I'm letting this get the best of me. I just want to turn off my caring because when I don't think about it I feel a lot better—at least until I try to go to sleep."

When we explored what was causing Jim the most suffering, it was actually how bad he felt about feeling bad. "I hate being a wimp about this, and I'm sick of the conflict it's causing with my current wife because she gets mad every time Mike hurts me, and I find myself defending him, which then makes her madder."

Jim's struggle to accept his pain contributed to his feelings of shame about the whole situation. "I don't talk about this to friends because it feels embarrassing. I worry that they'll think less of me, and when I toy with bringing this up at church for others to pray about, I never do because I don't really want them to know."

Jim's desire to keep his feelings from others is an example of Jacob Needleman's observation that we can fall into "making a religion of our better moments."[2] Like Jim, sometimes we don't know how to bring our vulnerable and imperfect parts into our relationships with others, let alone how to weave this thread into our perceptions of who we are. It can feel easier to try to push these feelings away in hopes of becoming the people we think we're supposed to be.

Almost without exception, I see this dynamic when I sit with people who are talking about emotional pain. After describing their feelings, they add on a trailer of self-criticism for feeling the way they do.

"I know it's stupid."

"I realize how silly this is."

"It's embarrassing to even admit this has gotten me so worked up."

As with Jim, it's these afterthoughts of self-judgment that make already-difficult times even more difficult. For whatever reason, most of us have a built-in reflex to kick ourselves, or at least to minimize the validity of our emotions, when we're feeling down.

Maybe some of this stems from moments we've lived that are similar to what I witnessed at a department store the other day. There was a small girl wailing quite loudly. In an effort to quiet her, her grandmother got down on her knees, looked her right in the eyes, and said, "Suzy, there are a lot of happy people in here, and happy people don't want to hear the sounds of a person crying because that doesn't make them happy. They don't like it, and they don't want to hear you."

While I have to admit that my eardrums agreed with the grandmother's words, another part of me wanted to intervene and say, "Actually, I don't mind if you cry. Go ahead and feel however you want to feel."

Mostly, I want to announce this message to all of the places within each of us where we hold the belief that we're better off not feeling what we feel—those parts of us that take on the role of guards, tapping their clubs in warning at the slightest hint of any unattractive emotions.

Often, underlying this stance is the assumption that we should be having a different experience than we are. In these moments, it's helpful to imagine the possibility that what we're feeling isn't an error. Possibly, our emotional hardwiring is precisely accurate in how it responds to what we live through. As one of my friends likes to say, "I would have a different story to tell if my experience had been different." The same goes with our emotions. More often than not, what we feel makes a lot of sense given what we've experienced and how it's affected us.

To embrace our emotions, it helps to see that often the experiences that bring us to our knees are also what allow us to grow into the fullness of who we really are. I'm reminded of Rumi's description of this paradox in his poem "The Question." As he describes,

One group walks toward the fire, *into* the fire, another
toward the sweet flowing water.
No one knows which are blessed and which not.
Whoever walks into the fire appears suddenly in the
    stream.
A head goes under on the water surface, that head
pokes out of the fire . . .
The trickery goes further.
The voice of the fire tells the *truth* saying, *I am not fire.*
I am fountainhead. Come into me and don't mind the
    sparks.[3]

The same truth holds for the fire of painful feelings. Sometimes their presence is a gift in disguise. This complexity relates to the idea of the *trickster,* the force in life that arrives in unexpected ways, shaking us out of our secure and reasoned sense of how things are and how things should be. One only has to walk a labyrinth to be reminded of this trickster energy. At the beginning of this maze-like spiral, we find ourselves moving directly to the center of the circle, thinking our journey will be quick and simple. Unexpectedly, the path then takes us all the way to the outer circumference, requiring us to work our way back to the middle, turn by turn and loop by loop. In moments, we can think we're making progress only to have the next bend take us back to ground that, seemingly, we've already traveled. At some point, when we feel the farthest away from the center, the path ushers us right into our destination.

This same dynamic applies to our journey with emotions. By moving into them, feeling into their depths, we can come to free ourselves from their grip. Thus, if we can allow ourselves to feel fully, cry deeply, and follow the thread of our grief completely, we're much better able to move through difficult times and resurface with a sense of freshness in our life.

This was essential for Jim in healing his relationship with his son. First, Jim committed to honestly sitting with his pain, noticing what it felt like in his body and following this trail of sensations. He noticed a feeling of almost unbearable heat in his chest. As I encouraged him to observe this *unbearable* quality, he came to see that beneath it was a profound level of guilt for the years he hadn't been actively involved as a father. Tears streamed down his cheeks as he felt his sadness about missing out on time with his son and letting him down by his absence. "I've never apologized," he sobbed. "I guess I just hoped that, if I began to show up, I could make things right without having to look at what I did. I think I've been scared to say I'm sorry—scared to own up to what was my fault because I don't think I can forgive myself, let alone expect him to."

We explored what it would look like to not bury these feelings again—to truly own his regret and honestly share his realizations with his son. This became the first step in healing their relationship and a huge step for Jim in understanding the value of sitting with the truth of his feelings.

Sometimes with clients it's enough to simply introduce the idea that we can lean into our emotions and that this creates a cleaner path than getting caught in a web of judgment and criticism about how we feel. At other times I introduce a practice based on the principles of *tonglen* meditation[4] as a way of reversing our tendencies to push away what we don't want to feel.

As with Jim, I encourage people to notice where they feel emotional pain in their physical body and to tune into what sensations, such as heat and heaviness, accompany this pain. Sometimes it helps to first close our eyes or soften our gaze and take a few deep breaths. It can also be useful to review some of the details surrounding the situation that's causing pain. After a minute or so, we then let go of these details, in a sense dropping beneath them, in order to connect more directly with the sensations connected to our feelings.

In the practice of *tonglen,* one imagines breathing in these difficult sensations and feelings, intentionally taking them in and being present with them as an encouragement to counteract our typical response of pushing them away. The point of the practice, which is both simple and challenging, is to allow ourselves to feel what we feel. To support this, when we notice our mind starting to replay images of the events that happened we gently redirect our attention back to the feelings in our body.

It can help if we imagine embracing our emotions the same way a loving parent embraces a child, with a sense of acceptance and a willingness to notice and allow the presence of these feelings. As we do this, we can begin to notice how our experience shifts—if it becomes more or less intense, or if new emotions arise.

Once we've felt these feelings, we can move into the second aspect of *tonglen* by imagining that, on our exhalation, we're breathing out a sense of lightness and ease. *Tonglen,* which means "sending and taking," is traditionally done in sync with the breath— breathing in the sensations that are connected to our painful emotions and breathing out what we imagine to be the opposite quality. On the out-breath, we imagine this quality permeating through and around us, offering balance to our felt sense of difficulty.

It can also be powerful to engage in this practice, not only at a personal level but also in a more universal way—recognizing that as we breathe in our own pain there are many other people experiencing similar difficulty. We can then imagine that as we exhale we're sending out relief not only to ourselves but also to others. In this way, the meditation practice allows our pain to connect us to others by reminding us of our common humanity.

I've had this experience while driving, feeling in a rush to get to my destination while also responding to the needs of my children. I remember, on one occasion, breathing into this feeling of being overwhelmed, surrendering to its presence, and looking over to the next lane to see another mother living out her version of this same challenging and ordinary moment. I breathed out a sense of ease for both of us.

Such experiences are gifts in allowing us to see that, even in our individual distress, we're participating in something larger than ourselves. I feel this appreciation when I watch dozens of children scamper out to the bus stop in the wee hours of the morning, imagining the similar mornings we've all lived through—the complexity of tasks involved in making it possible to engage in the simple act of catching the bus.

By embracing our painful feelings, we allow these moments of recognition to then open us to the fullness of our human experience and our connection to the world around us. In this lies another trickster reality: when we allow ourselves to be pierced and cracked open by life, we develop considerable hardiness because we no longer need to guard against the fear that we can't handle life's challenges. By showing up to face our difficulties, we gain confidence that we're capable of living through whatever life brings our way, and this strength then dissolves the scary monsters in the closet.

I recall a difficult day when I was talking to a friend. At the time, my professional life felt like it was narrowing, and I was rocked by the challenge of attempting to reconcile my intuitive sense of how things might open up and my lived experience of closing doors. I was sharing how shattered I felt, not only in my current predicament but also in how it was causing me to question my sense of knowing and my understanding of how things work in the world. As my friend handed me tissues, he said, "Well, if you're going to let this shatter you, just make sure to let it shatter you completely. It's always depressing to me to see people who are only partially broken."

I couldn't help but laugh at his comment and look at him with some puzzlement. "What do you mean by that—it depresses you?"

He went on to explain his observation that people who get partially broken tend to build up more defenses and ego to protect their crack. "But if you're fully broken open, then you're just open. It's much cleaner that way."

I've come to see his point and to understand how this willingness to be pierced open by even the moments in life that we desperately don't want does in fact bring a sort of awakening to our being that isn't otherwise possible. This awareness allows us to respond to the shattering of *who we think we are* with a bow of reverence for the spiritual gift of unraveling the truth of *who we really are*.

Practice

- What difficult emotions do you tend to push away? What feeling do you wish you would never have to experience again? Why?

- How might you begin to develop a sense of hardiness in your ability to feel the sensations associated with this emotion?

  - Is there someone who could hold space for you to explore the monster-like qualities of these feared emotions?

  - Would it be useful to experiment with your own version of *tonglen,* breathing into your feelings and exhaling the opposite quality?

  - Can you connect to the truth that other humans share this same pain?

- What have been the tricksters in your life? What has caused you to be shattered? Have you found unexpected gifts in these unwanted situations?

KNOWING, ACCEPTING, AND BEFRIENDING OURSELVES

*What arises in our experience is much less important than
how we relate to what arises in our experience.*

— MARK EPSTEIN

Given how common it is for us to push aside what
we don't want to feel and to judge ourselves for feeling
that way, it's worth exploring a bit more about what
it looks like to truly support ourselves during difficult
times. While it's wonderful to receive care from friends
and loved ones when we're going through challenges,
I'm often struck by how little attention is given to how
we care for ourselves—or don't care for ourselves—
during times like these.

To begin, it helps to think about the steps we might
take in making a commitment to someone else. First,
we'd want to come to know them quite well and to
work toward accepting them for who they are. We'd
also want to learn how to be a good friend to them—
understanding their vulnerabilities and how best to
offer them love and support. These same steps of *knowing, accepting,* and *befriending* apply to becoming good
companions to ourselves.

While this observation may seem quite obvious
and easy to agree with in good times, sometimes these
qualities quickly go out the window when we're face-
to-face with our limits and flaws. It would be great if we
were encouraged early on in life to make some sort of

internal vow, committing to stay supportive and true to ourselves through thick *and* thin.

Such fidelity to oneself is easier to sustain once we've come to know ourselves more deeply by contacting the rocky terrain of our interior—learning more about the places where we feel tender so that we can develop our strength, not separate from this but rather by including these aspects of ourselves. This relationship between embracing difficulty and moving toward self-acceptance reminds me of a massage I once experienced in which the practitioner first worked very deeply, massaging the abdominal organs with the understanding that only by releasing tension at this internal level could the surface stomach muscles feel secure enough to soften in their protective role.

I found this approach fascinating in the way it applies to diving into difficult emotions as a means of freeing up our capacity to be more fully open to the breadth of who we are. While the massage therapist helped me see the places of vulnerability in my physical body, my exploration of my inner self has helped me understand the places where I feel emotionally tender.

Engaging in this type of process is important for all of us. I've yet to meet anyone who doesn't have this vulnerable dimension of their inner life; however, the universality of these experiences is often surprising to people. My own version of this surprise came when, as a teenager, I was reading a psychology text. It stated that all humans, at their core, want to be loved and to feel like they have something to offer. The text went on to describe how people want to know that they're enough and that they likely have pockets of insecurity about this, whether these pockets are perched right at the surface of their skin or held deep down near their internal organs.

When I read this description, I felt disappointed because it so accurately summed up what I knew to be true about myself. As a teenager, I had come to think that the inner workings of my psyche were sophisticated and unique, possibly incomprehensible to any other human. But here the text was telling me that what I'd encountered inside myself was, in fact, quite ordinary.

Since then, as I've continued to see versions of these same vulnerabilities in others, I've often wished there could be some cultural movement to normalize their presence. If this were to happen, it might be easier for us to accept and support all of who we are and to not feel embarrassed or judgmental of these places inside. It's as if the whole world walks around feeling hesitant to whisper their secrets: "I want to be loved. I want to do well. I feel vulnerable about these things." It would be so much easier if we could come to the planet with inscribed wristbands that could let us know from an early age: "You are not alone in this." Maybe this truth could be included in our pledges of allegiance, so we can get it out in the open. "One people, under God, united by our vulnerability . . . " with, I hope, some strength and resiliency as well.

People of all ages feel the tug of these vulnerabilities: wanting to fit in socially, wanting to have love reciprocated, wanting to be appreciated by family, wanting to be acknowledged at work, wanting intimacy, wanting to be accepted, wanting to feel pretty enough, wanting to feel capable of tackling the demands of daily life, of overcoming fears, or of feeling strong enough to continue functioning in the face of depression or illness.

As we uncover these inner places, they often reflect writer Esther Hautzig's observation that "feelings are untidy."[5] They also present an opportunity to see the wisdom in psychiatrist Mark Epstein's idea that how we relate to the inner messiness of these feelings is what's most important.

I often encourage people to consider the possibility that's it's okay to be humbled. Just as with difficult emotions, we're often wired and raised to steer clear of situations that make us feel vulnerable and small—instead, pursuing things that make us feel grander. Fortunately, most of us, however, can afford to let life's sandpaper smooth our edges. We can handle being diminished on occasion if we know deep down that our survival isn't at stake. It can even feel refreshing to allow ourselves to be amused at not winning, being proven wrong, or being made a fool of—well, okay, maybe only a slight fool. If we've allowed ourselves to be shattered, such insults to the ego are more tolerable.

One of my personal versions of mild sandpaper involved a trip to the grocery store on a day when I didn't have time to deal with the small details of life beforehand. As I set off, with unwashed hair clipped up on my head—accompanied by my two young children and a stain of smashed green beans on my sweatshirt—I soon realized that I'd better start embracing my imperfections. As much as I wanted to be able to appear capable and competent, it suddenly seemed pointless to attempt to publically present myself as a health professional who had all the answers or as someone who had transcended the awkwardness of day-to-day life. On that day, my realness was all too visible.

By aisle three, my daughter was crying and I was spitting on her pacifier to clean off pocket fuzz and floor dust, before putting it back in her mouth. My son beheld a bottle of green catsup and, after my initial reaction of disgust, I found myself merrily giving it to him to hold, as if this carried some insurance that aisles four through twelve would go smoothly. By aisle six, he was screaming, "Donut, donut," at the top of his lungs. Usually he's shy and doesn't speak loudly. Why now? Soon, my cart was full of coping mechanisms: a six-pack of beer, expensive chocolate, fully caffeinated coffee. Even in my attempts to conceal them amid the organic produce and tofu, their sheer volume made them conspicuous.

Of course, this was the day that I ran into all sorts of people I knew: a colleague from the university dressed in professional attire, a client who had previously held me in high regard ("Dr. Horneffer, is that you?"), and a health-conscious friend whose children had never been introduced to the word *donut,* let alone tasted one to know it was an item worth crying out for.

I was humbled, to say the least, and I had to surrender to the reality that life was forcing me to see and show all of who I was. It took some time for me to see that these ordinary and challenging moments of day-to-day life have value in rubbing us into becoming more authentic. Over time, I've come to think that maybe this is the way life loves us into becoming more real—a different version of what the tattered skin horse had tried to explain to the Velveteen Rabbit.

The experience of busyness can hold this same sandpaper quality. It often forces us to give up our attempts to be superheroes because we finally meet our match in terms of what we can handle. One day when I was walking into my university office, with two heavy bags strapped around my shoulders, I encountered a graduate student who worked in our department.

"Can I help you carry that?" he asked.

"No," I responded, "I've got it."

"Of course you do," he chimed back. "You like to be Superwoman."

I laughed as I dismissed the idea, but then he quickly added, "Well then, I will be Robin."

Hmmm . . .

In Arlie Hochschild's book *The Second Shift,* she writes: "When I show my students a picture of the woman with the flying hair, briefcase in one hand, child in the other, they say she is unreal, but they want to be just like her."[6] I had been somewhat successful in denying this desire within myself until my Superwoman moment. Maybe it was something about the fantasy of trading in my minivan for the Batmobile or, better yet, the invisible plane. Maybe, too, it was something about getting a *Robin* thrown into the package that allowed the floodgates of my longing to burst open.

Whatever the reason, it was a moment of insight. I realized, first, that I had this desire and, second, that the fullness of my life was preventing me from pulling off my heroic presentation whether in the grocery store, my work setting, or the caverns of my own heart. This happens for all of us sooner or later. Eventually, the too much–ness of life finally forces us to take off our capes. For me, it was important to see that by assuming I should always have a cape on I wasn't honoring the places in me that felt no desire to be heroic—the places that simply wanted to rest and accept my imperfection.

Embracing our vulnerabilities is doable, and it helps if we can find tools for staying in conversation with all these aspects of who we are. We need ways of contacting our limitations and strengths, and whatever else we might find inside, without drowning in the intensity of what's there. For some people, writing in a journal serves as a wonderful way to access our inner life. For visual people, drawing, painting, and creating collages can be similar doorways to exploring the breadth of who we are.

I've been honored to witness extraordinary creations—from heartfelt diary entries to painted images of people bowing to the earth while being illuminated by moonlight from above. I've been moved when seeing collections of powerful quotes and images pasted together to reflect the complexity and richness of the inner life. These expressions are sacred in how they convey the depth of the human experience.

For Sarah, movement and dance were her ways of expressing what she felt inside. She found a local group of women interested in gathering monthly to move to music as a means of embodying whatever emotions wanted to come through. In very different ways, Lisa's decision to start a blog for mothers with autistic children and Carol's participation in an Internet group for single parents served the same goal. These women created their own ways to connect with others and to express the layers of emotions and uncertainties they were grappling with. Support groups, psychotherapy, psycho-educational classes, and women's and men's groups can serve this same purpose.

By enabling us to express ourselves, these types of experiences allow us to deepen our trust in what we feel. They also allow us to stay present with ourselves and to stay true to whatever self-commitment we choose to make.

As we consider making an inner vow, it helps to take some time to reflect on the deeper qualities within ourselves that we want to support and stay aligned with. I love how Oriah Mountain Dreamer's poem "The Invitation" asks the sorts of questions that lead us to what's most essential by stripping away the distracting, superficial details of daily life. As she conveys in the opening lines of her poem:

> It doesn't interest me what you do for a
> living. I want to know what you ache for,
> and if you dare to dream of meeting your
> heart's longing.
> It doesn't interest me how old you are. I want
> to know if you will risk looking like a fool

for love, for your dream, for the adventure
of being alive. . .[7]

She then goes on to ask:

> I want to know if you can see beauty, even
>   when it is not pretty, every day, and if you
>   can source your own life from its presence.
> I want to know if you can live with failure,
>   yours and mine, and still stand at the edge
>   of the lake and shout to the silver of the
>   full moon, *"Yes!"*

As we think about making a commitment to ourselves, this is the type of inner conversation we need to
have. Not that we have to be this poetic—but it can be
useful to reflect on what versions of these questions are
worth asking ourselves, just as we might ask of another
or have that other ask of us. What is it that feels most
important to commit to in your life and within yourself?

Practice

- Play with the language from Oriah Mountain
  Dreamer's poem and write some questions to
  yourself. What comes to mind when you think of
  the phrase "It doesn't interest me . . . I want to
  know . . . "?

- Consider writing a vow to yourself. What would
  you want to say, *at the altar,* if you were to

marry yourself? What commitments do you want
to make?

- What areas of vulnerability are you aware of?
  How do you respond to their presence?

- What would it look like to accept and befriend
  yourself in moments when you feel humbled
  by life?

- What tools help you to be in conversation with
  yourself: journaling, artistic expression,
  movement, communicating with others either in
  person or online?

REMEMBERING KINDNESS

*. . . Before you know kindness as the deepest thing inside,
you must know sorrow as the other deepest thing . . .*

— NAOMI SHIHAB NYE

Although the topics of difficulty and kindness don't
necessarily seem related at first glance, they end up having an important thread that connects them. Not only
do we need to know difficulty to know genuine kindness, as Nye suggests, but as she goes on to describe, it's
often kindness that offers a way forward when we've
confronted difficulty:

You must wake up with sorrow.
You must speak to it till your voice

catches the thread of all sorrows
and you see the size of the cloth.

Then it is only kindness that makes any sense anymore,
only kindness that ties your shoes
and sends you out into the day to mail letters and
      purchase bread . . .[8]

A brief anecdote honoring the life of Kobun Chino Otogawa Roshi conveys a similar idea. It describes his response to a visibly distraught woman in the audience at one of his talks soon after the attack on the World Trade Center. She asked, "How can I deal with the enormous fear and anger that I feel about what happened?"

Kobun replied, "Do one kind thing for someone every day."[9]

As Sharon Salzberg points out, "It is easy to overlook the power of kindness or misunderstand it."[10] I'm sure there were people in the audience of Kobun's talk that day who didn't expect his response. "Kindness? Are you kidding?" Even to people who embrace kindness, such encouragement can seem ignorant, soft, and possibly even wimpy. What's important to understand is that such gestures aren't merely ways of distracting ourselves from our emotional pain. They represent a powerful choice we end up making when we're confronted with sorrow, anger, injustice, or disappointment: the choice of whether we're going to shut down or allow these experiences to become an inner fertilizer that can strengthen our capacity to open our hearts to ourselves and to those around us.

Just as confronting difficulty can cause us to shut down, so can having too many demands on our plate. While stress can snuff out our inherent flame of kindness, it's in these times that we most need such light. On the one hand, we can think of this in moral terms—how it's always a good thing to be a generous person who thinks of others. Sometimes, what's harder to see is that we need to feel connected to our own kindness for our *own* well-being, especially when our lives are full and our time seems completely spent.

In these moments, we need kindness in the form of self-compassion so that we can be gentle with ourselves when we've bitten off more than we can chew. We also need it in the form of staying connected to our natural instincts to be kind toward others because feeling moved to be thoughtful or generous toward someone else offers the gift of pulling us out of our myopic self-focus. When we genuinely desire to ease someone's pain, make someone's day, or contribute our voice to a cause we care about, we give ourselves access to a store of energy that wouldn't otherwise be available. The relevance of such gestures reminds me of philosopher Dan Dennett's words: "The secret of happiness: Find something more important than you are and dedicate your life to it."[11] By finding our *something* through kindness and care for others we can open up a new way of being in relationship to life experiences that can otherwise feel unbearable.

Our innate capacity to be kind and generous can also get extinguished by the presence of busyness. Ask any parent about the times when they're most likely to lose their temper with their children or to become hypercritical of themselves. This same dynamic plays out everywhere—just observe the interaction between people and the clerk in the checkout line at a grocery store. When not rushed, shoppers are kind, laughing, and treating the clerks as humans. Yet when busy, these shoppers lose this awareness, treating the clerks as mere pawns in their grand attempt to finish errands.

I hate to admit that I sometimes do this, too, when I'm in a hurry to get out of a store or to get my check at a restaurant. How much harder it is in these moments to find kindness inside. In contrast, there was a day this summer when I took my children out for lunch. It was a fairly open, unscheduled afternoon and we had plenty of time before we needed to be anywhere. As we sat down, a woman at the next table asked our names. She was both friendly and a little awkward in her style of interacting. At some point, she mentioned that she had taken a bus to the restaurant and actually lived in a community shelter a few miles away. Then, a few sentences later, she inquired about the cost of the food we were eating. I couldn't help but ask if I could buy her a sandwich.

She enthusiastically answered yes, and we ordered the combination of ingredients she wanted. Soon after, she asked me, "Where do you go to church?" As I responded to her question, I realized I wasn't really answering her question. It seemed that she wanted to know where my kindness came from, and although this has been encouraged at the churches I've attended, she'd have to follow a long thread back into the early years of my life to understand the full answer to her question.

She'd have to know the church of the minister who comforted my mom when she lost her two-week-old son, assuring her that he wasn't going to hell for not being baptized, as another minister had told her. She'd need to have known my mother as well, and the many people who came up to me at her funeral, introducing themselves as people she had been kind to. She'd have to meet my father, who befriends almost every human being within minutes of meeting them, regardless of their demographic profile. She'd have to meet my sixth-grade teacher and several of my high school teachers, along with professors in college and graduate school who inspired me to be kind. She'd also have to meet the people I've encountered and known who haven't been kind and have influenced me to be otherwise.

Of course, such a thread exists for each of us, and it's powerful to reflect on what events and actions have informed our choices to be compassionate or to withhold compassion. As I once heard author Wayne Muller ask, "What is the smallest act of kindness anyone has ever done for you that made the biggest difference?"

Along with reflecting on such questions, it's also worth considering our current relationship to kindness and how we might keep this capacity close by as an antidote to life's difficulty. Some people have a much easier time being compassionate toward others than toward themselves. When I hear people being highly self-critical, I often ask if this is the way they'd speak to a friend or family member they love. Typically people chuckle at the ridiculousness of this: "Of course not. I'd never be that mean to someone else!" For those of us who need to enter the kindness equation by first focusing on how we show up with ourselves, it's helpful to apply a twist to the Golden Rule. Along with "doing unto others as we'd have others do unto us," we should commit to "doing unto ourselves as we do unto others." Sometimes it's useful to imagine offering ourselves the same kindness that we extend to a loved one.

Considering the value of kindness brings up the question of why we humans have the capacity to be unkind at all—toward ourselves or others. Sometimes, we become self-critical because we've internalized the voice of a significant person in our life who repeatedly verbalized criticisms toward us.

For Beth, this person was her father. As she shared, "I could bring home all A's and one B on my report card, and all I'd hear is, 'What happened?'"

For Alison, it was her private swimming coach. "The better I got the worse I felt about myself because the pressure he created was intolerable. By the time I qualified for nationals, I had learned to hate myself because the only comments that played in my head were the insults from my coach."

In Stephanie's case, her inner critic was a reflection of the voices of both her mother and ex-husband. "I think my mom was so obsessed with her appearance that she couldn't help but pass her judgments on to me. They were subtle comments, and I think she meant well in wanting me to be thin, but after gaining weight with my first pregnancy and hearing the same comments all over again from my husband, it was hard for me to feel good about my body and myself."

For all three women, the source of these inner criticisms wasn't initially obvious to them, even though these messages were with them on most days. For each of them, however, when asked to reflect on whose voice they were hearing in their head they quickly identified who in their life had offered similar remarks.

Sometimes these judgmental inner voices keep us from embracing our vulnerabilities because of how quick they are to criticize. The inner conflict created by this dynamic can cause a lockdown that prevents us from being able to access our capacity for self-compassion. This same dynamic can also keep us from being kind to others.

Beth became upset when she found herself imposing the same pressures on her son in regard to his grades. "I didn't say anything when he handed me his report card, but I know he saw it in my face. It's just hard for me not to expect what was expected of me." Stephanie felt the influence of others' comments about her weight when she found herself being critical toward people who were heavy. "I feel mean because I get so judgmental, but I can see I'm just imposing the same criteria on them that I'm putting on myself."

Sometimes we become judgmental not because we've been the recipient of criticisms directed at us but because we've seen this coping strategy used by others in our younger years. I remember a boy who often got in trouble at school for saying mean things to other kids. On several occasions, I heard his mother gossiping about others and talking poorly about several staff members at the school. On one occasion, I overheard her say, "I just don't understand why Tommy is so hard on the other kids . . ."

Regardless of whether we've been the recipient or observer of harsh criticism, identifying the source of these critical voices within ourselves expands our capacity to extend compassion toward ourselves and others. Sometimes this is enough. For Alison, it was essential that she put her coach's face to the beliefs she was carrying around. This allowed her to realize that a part of her, emotionally, was stuck back in time and needed to be reassured that this period of her life was over.

Beth needed to look at not only the source of her criticisms but also the way she had internalized them and brought them into her parenting. With such explorations, it's useful to assume that when we fuel critical voices something in our system believes that adopting this judgment is helpful. With this in mind, I asked Beth to consider what this critical voice wanted for her son and what this voice feared would happen if it didn't hold this high standard for him. After pausing, she explained, "When I'm being critical, really my intention is that I want him to be successful and happy, and I worry that if I don't push him, he's not going to understand that his grades can make a difference in getting into college and having a successful career."

By clarifying this, Beth was able to brainstorm other ways she could support her son while being more loving in her interactions. "Maybe I need to have a heart-to-heart talk with him so he understands that my encouragement comes out of wanting what's best for him. I could also create some rewards for all his good grades."

Stephanie's process was similar in that we asked the same questions regarding the part of her that felt critical toward her body. Because her judgments were self-directed, we asked what this part of herself wanted *for herself.*

"I don't want my weight to get out of hand. I think I'm scared that if I stop being hard on myself, I'll ditch my exercise program and forget to eat moderately."

Together, we explored what it would be like for this voice to take on a less extreme form, trusting that it wasn't the sole inner torchbearer for her health and vitality. "It never occurred to me that I could trust in my enjoyment of exercise and my history of making good choices about my eating. Somehow, I think this critical voice assumed it was the glue holding everything together."

Although some people might be considered incapable of acting kindly toward others due to characteristics that can be diagnosed as narcissistic or sociopathic, the strong majority of human beings not only are capable of being generous but also thrive on tapping into their reservoir of compassion and generosity. By living from this place, we come to know our potential for making a difference in the world around us and for creating a life of meaning. Typically, when people are cut off from this potential it's due to some inner tension similar to that lived by Beth, Alison, and Stephanie. It can also stem from not having had opportunities to find their own blueprint for what genuine kindness looks and feels like. As children, we're often encouraged to be nice and play nice before we've really discovered what it means to be kind to ourselves and to extend this to others. Such encouragements don't always allow us to develop an authentic relationship to our inherent kindness.

It's important that we find our own ways of being kind and compassionate, in part, so that we don't end up merely shutting down in response to the many requests for our generosity that regularly arrive. Over the past few days, I've been asked to give money to seven organizations, to host someone at my house and to let another person move in, to give blood, to join a committee that lost a member, to join a sports league that has an injured player, to buy magazines and chocolate bars for a fund-raiser, to give money to an elementary school for children who run a certain number of laps and to a preschool for laps completed on a tricycle, to provide a snack for 80 children, to chip in for a gift, to offer supervision to an intern, to proofread a newsletter, and to take in an aggressive dog and a stray cat.

While all of these causes and situations are important and meaningful, I'm reminded of my inclination to duck behind cafeteria tables rather than having to say "no"—because it's too much to say "yes" to everyone. It's important that we don't become so overwhelmed by these sorts of requests that we lose our ability to be generative in our kindness in small and large ways that feel authentic and meaningful. I often encourage people to think of how they'd like to make a difference in the world around them because such proactive thoughts and efforts can be especially life-giving and fulfilling.

Kindness, in the form of forgiveness, is particularly powerful. Certainly, cultivating forgiveness is a process that can't be forced. The journey of arriving at such a place takes both time and an understanding of what forgiveness is and isn't. Sometimes forgiveness is misunderstood as being about condoning what happened or opening oneself up to harm. Instead, it helps to see forgiveness as a willingness to reclaim and free up emotional energy that otherwise becomes stagnant and sour when we stew in anger and resentment. Of all the ways I've seen people stay stuck in negativity, being unable or unwilling to move toward forgiveness is most notable—regardless of whether this involves marriages, partnerships, collegial relationships, friendships, parents, children, or oneself.

At the same time, forgiveness is one of the best ways to gain back the time and energy that's otherwise lost to resentment. I understand that forgiveness isn't always possible between individuals or groups. Sometimes we feel that the harm done to us or done by us is too great to move past. I encourage people, however, to at least experiment with holding the intention to some- day choose and be capable of setting down grudges and feeling open to forgive. When holding this intention doesn't feel possible or of value, it can at least become a trailhead, leading to an understanding of why we feel the need to hold on to anger. When we walk this trail, we often see that withholding forgiveness doesn't nec- essarily protect us. In fact, when we stake out territory in our heart to house resentment, anger, or hate we end up losing more of our life energy to the very person or situation that we want to be free from.

The act of forgiveness and other gestures of kindness are empowering because they allow us to have an impact on the world around us. This is the brilliance of Kobun's suggestion to do one kind thing a day. Under such circumstances, generosity becomes a way of overcoming bitterness and having some control of a situation in which we can otherwise feel powerless.

Practice

- What is the connection between kindness and difficulty in your own life?

- What would it look and feel like to be kind to yourself in your day-to-day life, especially when you next encounter pain or difficulty?

- If you notice the presence of critical inner voices, see if you can identify where they come from. Notice, also, what these critical voices want for you and what they're concerned might happen if they don't voice their judgment.

- Reflect on how kindness shows up in your interactions with others.

    - Can you think of a small act of kindness that made a big difference in your life?

    - In what ways do you feel drawn to offer kindness to others?

- Do you notice a connection between compassion and busyness in your daily life? When you initially feel too busy to be compassionate, what can you do to shift that feeling? Sometimes this awareness alone can help us remember that kindness is always an option.

Given that difficulty is inevitable, it's worth finding ways not only to cope with the challenging aspects of life but also to use them as opportunities for finding our strength, accepting all of who we are, and deepening our sense of compassion for others. When we confront vulnerabilities and limitations within ourselves, rather than trying to push them away, I find it's more fruitful to embrace them with a sense of acceptance and curiosity. Often, the more we open to these places within, the more we're able to respond to life's challenges with confidence, wisdom, and kindness.

FINDING
BALANCE IN
THE SWIRL

For everything you have missed, you have
gained something else, and for everything
you gain, you lose something else.

— RALPH WALDO EMERSON

If we're successful in carving out a meaningful life, it's likely that our life will seem too busy and too much from time to time. For most of us, if we had to err in one direction or the other, we really wouldn't want it to be otherwise—we want to feel like we're making the most of our lives and helping to make a difference in the lives of those around us. I remember receiving an e-mail one day that signed off: "Enjoy the Swirl." The phrase struck me as a reminder to show up and, to whatever degree possible, delight in the fullness of each day. I saw this phrase as a motivation to recognize the preciousness contained in the ordinary and extraordinary moments of life. It made me think of Thoreau's desire "to not, when I come to die, discover that I have not lived . . . to live deep and suck out all the marrow of life."[1]

It's useful to imagine what it might be like when we near the end of our life and look back on our days. I often think it will be the very small things that I'll most appreciate and miss—glancing up to see a full moon in the evening sky, tucking my kids in at night, offering a kind word to someone, laughing with a friend over some small occurrence. I remember, a few years ago, when my husband and I were sprinting into a poetry reading, running late because we had needed to drop our kids off somewhere. As I started getting stressed, my husband commented, "It doesn't really matter if we're late to the reading. You know, we're living the poem right here."

I loved his recognition of the delicious swirl in that moment, and I imagine I'll look back on that day later in my life as another small yet precious memory. I'm also aware that between now and then I'll forget all of this many times. I'll forget to name the swirl as a swirl, to think of life as having marrow, and to feel grateful for any of it.

This tendency to forget is true for most of us, particularly when the backdrop of our lives is fullness and busyness. I've come to see that any journey we take around living consciously, growing personally, or serving others is inevitably influenced by our dance of forgetting and remembering—and then forgetting and remembering again. Maybe it's not that we ever fully forget, but our awareness of our intentions ebbs and flows as the demands of life tug us in different directions.

These rhythms of showing up fully and getting knocked off-balance are not that different from the movements of ocean waves as they rush onto shore and withdraw into the sea. They're an inherent part of life, and any conversation about finding balance or nourishing ourselves needs to take this ebb and flow into account.

These currents end up affecting almost every dimension of our lives—including our capacity for honoring our rhythms, turning within, filling up, fully inhabiting our days, remembering lightness, and embracing difficulty. Given this reality, it's useful to imagine wrapping all these tools into a large net of compassion, remembering that perfection isn't really possible and isn't even the goal. Instead, it's more useful to have a goal of expanding ourselves enough to take in and appreciate the breadth of what life offers, along with all the ways we find ourselves showing up in this swirl.

I was presented with a wonderful metaphor for this breadth several years ago when my husband and I went out to eat at a small Mexican restaurant decorated with pepper-shaped lights that dangled from the ceiling. The owner soon arrived at our table with a plate of the house special balanced on his arm and several other plates resting on a tray just behind him.

"This dish," he said with a sparkle in his eye, "gets three 'Oh, my Gods.' First, for the seasoned chicken inside the enchilada—deeliciouuss—Oh, my God! Second, for the pistachio mole sauce drizzled on top. My grandfather's recipe. Oh . . . my . . . God! And then we have the mango chutney, our house specialty. Just look at it. You have all of life right here: the salty, the sweet, the spicy. Together, it gets a third 'Oh, my God.'"

"I'll take it!" I interrupted, without waiting to hear the other options. I wanted to add, "You had me at the chicken!" but it seemed my adoration was already apparent from the enthusiasm of my response. "This man is utterly delightful," I commented to my husband, "and he's just summed up the totality of the human experience with one plate of food." It was an image that stuck with me.

Soon after that amazing meal, I found God's name returning, as I looked out the snowy window of my counseling office and saw two beautiful deer walking by. "Oh, my God," I whispered slowly, feeling graced by such beauty. As I drove home from work, I saw that the two lighted reindeer we had placed in our front yard as a holiday decoration had blown over. "Oh, God!" I let out, not understanding why our family seemed to be punished for purchasing these one-step decorations. As I picked up our poor deer once again and got covered in the cold snow, I couldn't help but moan, "Shit!" under my breath. Why was it that every other deer, Santa, and sleigh I passed on the way home was standing erect and proud, whereas our front yard looked like a scene from a successful day of hunting?

As I was reflecting on those few days, I realized that when life is really good *God* gets a *my* and *shit* gets a *holy* and when life is annoying these words are left out. I know for myself that the longer I live, the more I continue to be amazed by life—in both good and bad ways. I've also noticed that the more I come to embrace and accept all the *Gods* and *shits*—with or without the *my* or *holy*—the more I can see life's beauty and appreciate just how expansive life really is. I've often thought that if there were a Book of Life, it would need to contain numerous foldout pages along the way. The ones where we think we're viewing the complete pictures until we open them up and see that there's actually much more going on to the left and to the right.

I find myself wanting to prepare my children, in an honest and delicate manner, for the fact that their days, too, will be filled with moments of inspiration and awe, as well as moments of profound disappointment. More than this, I want to assure them that all of life can be held in some cradle of *okayness*, even when they find themselves exclaiming, "It's not fair!" Whether this involves a last cookie or first turn, I want them to understand that life's lack of fairness doesn't make it a tragedy. Instead, those seemingly unfair times are simply aspects of the great block of wood from which each of us carves out our days. I want them to know that we all have to find our ways of making sense of life's complexities and paradoxes—how they, too, might turn to kindness as a response to life's difficulty.

It seems that incompatible dualities represent the ebb and flow in life. When we fail to embrace this larger perspective, we can find ourselves ping-ponging back and forth in our opinions and feelings about the occurrences that thread throughout our lives, "oohhing" and "ahhhing" with delight and discouragement at each twist and turn. Over the course of time, however, by taking an aerial view, we begin to realize that these events come together to weave an unexpectedly exquisite tapestry. It's just hard to see this at certain points in the chronology of our lives.

I think this is what C. S. Lewis was getting at when he said, in his grief over the loss of his wife, "The pain now is part of the happiness then."[2] They are inseparable, just as is described in the Buddhist notion of *interbeing*, which names the intertwined existence of various elements—much like the idea of *systems theory* in our culture. The raisin isn't separate from the grape, nor is it separate from the sunshine and water and soil that enabled the grape to grow. The raisin is also connected to the people who grow the grapes and to the people who dry it and put it in a box and those who drive it from vineyard to market. Simply by existing, every object contains a universe of other things within it.

This same complexity becomes apparent every April when dainty bright tulips seem to appear out of nowhere, as if they are springy balloons that have gently landed on the earth. Instead, of course, they first had to break through the hardened soil. They had to demonstrate a fiery warriorship to be in what now seems like a sweet, delicate position. Often, we are required to muster this type of determination to nourish our souls amid life's busyness and fullness.

These sorts of paradoxes are notably common in life. We labor, pushing from the depths of our being, to birth what is simply a natural expression of life. We then come to see that the same conditions that challenge us also reward us and open us more fully. Maybe this is why, in the Hindu faith, the deity Ganesha is seen as both the provider and remover of obstacles.

I hear clients struggle to come to terms with their own pushes and pulls, their own paradoxes in life, wondering how they can stretch themselves enough to embrace the range of what life offers them. All of us are faced with this task of remembering to stay connected with the big picture of our life—learning to embrace the sorts of shifts I've discussed—not only to help us get through life but also to help us live life fully and to ensure that our presence leaves a positive footprint on the world around us.

One day last fall as I was walking outside, returning from lunch to my office, the importance of this big-picture view came into clear focus. I had to reroute my path because of a large puddle at the bottom of a series of concrete steps. The puddle was filled with mud and brown leaves that created a murky, unattractive appearance. As I continued peering into this mess, however, my gaze came to the surface of the puddle, and I saw a reflection resting on top of the water. It was the most gorgeous image of a tree in its full autumn glory of oranges and yellows. The experience reminded me of a poster that at first looks like one image and then turns into something extraordinary as one's gaze softens. It was interesting that I could perceive both images with equal clarity; however, I could only see one image at a time. When I looked into the puddle and saw the mud and leaves, I could convince myself that this was reality. But, when I brought my attention to the surface, the reflection became real.

I took a breath and looked again to see if I could expand my sight to take in both realities. It felt like an exercise in opening to the mystery of paradox, to the possibility that multiple levels of reality co-exist. Here was an example, in nature, of ugliness and beauty being held in the same space. Interestingly, the ugliness helped to make the beauty more dramatic, maybe even to make it possible.

As I walked away, I reflected on the puddle. I began thinking about what being willing to *hold it all* means in my own life and in the lives of others. What does it look like to acknowledge that experiences of challenge and sorrow also hold seeds of growth and healing? What does it mean to realize that often what we perceive as unwanted events end up carrying essential threads throughout the fabric of our lives?

The image of the puddle also felt like an invitation to honor my own mud and leaves—to see that my limitations are also a part of the beauty of being human—to acknowledge all the ways they've served as a catalyst to wake me up more fully.

The experience was profound. It was a lot to get from one puddle. It confirmed my concerns that possibly I read too much into metaphors. But maybe not—because I've also come to see that when we're busy and trying to find balance in the swirl we have to grab hold of whatever moments of reflection and insight come our way. We must welcome them as part of our journey to find our own truths because we need such creative ways of staying in honest conversation with ourselves in order to find balance and nourishment for our souls. These conversations allow us to stay in connection with the essence of what all religions are about, *linking us back* to the truth of who we are and what life is about.

In the spirit of pausing with honesty, awareness, and compassion, it's important that we bow down to the breadth of our human experiences and to the larger mysteries that surround us. Seeing beauty in the swirls of life's busyness, making the most of what life brings our way, offering kindness to those around us, and being able to laugh from time to time. These gestures may be as grand as anything we can offer in our human life.

ENDNOTES

Tending to Our Thirst

Epigraph: From *Conjectures of a Guilty Bystander* by Thomas Merton, copyright © 1965, 1966 by the Abbey of Gethsemani. Used by permission of Doubleday, a division of Random House, Inc.

Shift 1: Honoring Our Rhythms

Epigraph: From *Sabbath: Restoring the Sacred Rhythm of Rest* by Wayne Muller, copyright © 1999 by Wayne Muller. Used by permission of Bantam Books, a division of Random House, Inc.

1. Ram Dass, *Spiritual Awakening* (Niles, IL: Nightingale-Conant, 1993).

   Epigraph: *Willy Wonka and the Chocolate Factory* (Paramount Pictures/Warner Brothers, 1971).

2. Mark Nepo, "Written While Running," in *Reduced to Joy*, copyright © 2007 by Mark Nepo. Used by permission of the author.

   Epigraph: Lynn Ungar, excerpt from "Camas Lilies," in *Blessing the Bread: Meditations by Lynn Ungar* (Boston: Unitarian Universalist Association, 1995).

3. From *Perseverance*, copyright © 2010 by Margaret Wheatley, Berrett-Koehler Publishers, Inc., San Francisco, CA. All rights reserved. Reprinted with permission of the publisher, www.bkconnection.com.

4. SARK, excerpt from "How to Really Love a Child," in *SARK's New Creative Companion* (Berkeley, CA: Ten Speed Press, 2005).

5. Reinhold Niebuhr, *The Essential Reinhold Niebuhr: Selected Essays and Addresses,* ed. Robert McAfee Brown (New Haven, CT: Yale University Press, 1987).

Shift 2: Turning Within

Epigraph: From *The Power of Myth* by Joseph Campbell & Bill Moyers, copyright © 1988 by Apostrophe S Productions, Inc. and Bill Moyers and Alfred Van der Marck Editions, Inc. for itself and the estate of Joseph Campbell. Used by permission of Doubleday, a division of Random House, Inc.

1. Stephan Rechtschaffen, *Timeshifting: Creating More Time to Enjoy Your Life* (New York: Doubleday, 1996).

2. David Whyte, *What to Remember When Waking* (Boulder, CO: Sounds True, 2010). Used by permission of Sounds True.

3. Antoine de Saint-Exupéry, *The Wisdom of the Sands* (New York: Harcourt Brace, 1950).

Epigraph: Quotation commonly attributed Blaise Pascal, adapted from *Pensées,* trans. W. F. Trotter, ed. A. Krailsheimer (New York: Penguin, 1966).

4. Lao Tzu, from Arthur Waley, *The Way and Its Power: A Study of the Tao Te Ching and Its Place in Chinese Thought* (London: Allen & Unwin, 1934).

5. Exercise adapted from Pir Vilayat Inayat Khan, *Awakening* (New York: Tarcher/Putnam, 1999).

6. From *Teaching a Stone to Talk: Expeditions and Encounters* by Annie Dillard. Copyright © 1982 by Annie Dillard. Reprinted by permission of HarperCollins Publishers.

7. Adyashanti, "Who Hears This Sound: Adyashanti on Waking Up from the Dream of Me," *The Sun* 384 (December 2007).

8. Jack Kornfield, *A Path with Heart: A Guide Through the Perils and Promises of Spiritual Life* (New York: Bantam, 1993).

Epigraph: Kobun Chino Otogawa Roshi, http://www
.everydaydharma.org/Kobun.html.

9. Judith Duerk, *I Sit Listening to the Wind: Woman's Encounter Within Herself* (San Diego, CA: LuraMedia, 1993).

10. From the book *Seven Whispers*. Copyright 2002 by Christina Baldwin. Reprinted with permission of New World Library, Novato, CA. www.newworldlibrary.com.

11. From *The Power of Myth* by Joseph Campbell & Bill Moyers, copyright © 1988 by Apostrophe S Productions, Inc. and Bill Moyers and Alfred Van der Marck Editions, Inc. for itself and the estate of Joseph Campbell. Used by permission of Doubleday, a division of Random House, Inc.

12. Kornfield, *A Path with Heart.*

13. Rumi, *The Illuminated Rumi,* trans. Coleman Barks, illuminations by Michael Green (New York: Broadway, 1997).

14. Elizabeth Gilbert, *Eat, Pray, Love: One Woman's Search for Everything Across Italy, India, and Indonesia* (New York: Penguin, 2006).

15. Kabir, in K. M. Sen, *Hinduism* (New York: Penguin, 2005).

Shift 3: Filling Up

Epigraph: Marianne Williamson, *Everyday Grace* (New York: Riverhead, 2002).

1. From *A Primer in Positive Psychology* by Christopher Peterson (2006). By permission of Oxford University Press, Inc.

Epigraph: Lao Tzu, commonly adapted verson based on *The Tao Te Ching of Lao Tzu,* trans. Brian Browne Walker (New York: St. Martin's Griffin, 1996).

2. J. O. Prochaska and W. F. Velicer, "The Transtheoretical Model of Health Behavior Change," *American Journal of Health Promotion* 12 (1997): 38–48; and J. Prochaska, "Change at Differing Stages," in *Handbook of Psychological Change:*

Psychotherapy Processes and Practices for the 21st Century, ed.
C. R. Snyder and R. E. Ingram (Hoboken, NJ: Wiley, 2000).

Epigraph: Erica Mann Jong, *Fear of Flying* (New York: Holt,
Rinehart & Winston, 1973).

3.   Richard Schwartz, *Internal Family Systems Therapy* (New York:
     Guilford Press, 1995).

Shift 4: Fully Inhabiting Our Days

Epigraph: Albert Einstein and Alice Calaprice, *The Ultimate
Quotable Einstein* (Princeton, NJ: Princeton University Press,
2010). Quotation attributed to Albert Einstein.

1.   Excerpted from *Real Happiness.* Copyright ©2010 by Sharon
     Salzberg. Used by permission of Workman Publishing Co., Inc.,
     New York. All rights reserved.

2.   Naomi Shihab Nye, "Valentine for Ernest Mann" from *Red
     Suitcase.* Copyright ©1994 by Naomi Shihab Nye. Reprinted
     with the permission of The Permissions Company, Inc. on
     behalf of BOA Editions Ltd., www.boaeditions.org.

Epigraph: Anne Lamott, *Bird by Bird: Some Instructions on
Writing and Life* (New York: Knopf Publishing Group, 1994).

3.   Parker Palmer, *Let Your Life Speak: Listening for the Voice of
     Vocation* (San Francisco: Jossey-Bass, 2000).

Epigraph: "The Gate," from *What the Living Do* by Marie
Howe. Copyright © 1997 by Marie Howe. Used by permission
of W. W. Norton & Company, Inc.

4.   Adapted from Angeles Arrien, Forward, *Maps to Ecstasy: A
     Healing Journey for the Untamed Spirit (Novato, CA: New World
     Library, 1998).*

Shift 5: Remembering Lightness

Epigraph: Rainer Maria Rilke, *Rilke's Book of Hours: Love Poems
to God,* trans. Anita Barrows and Joanna Macy (New York:

Riverhead, 2005).

1. Rainer Maria Rilke, *Letters to a Young Poet*, trans. Stephen Mitchell (New York: Modern Library, 2001).

   Epigraph: Howard Thurman in Gil Baile's *Violence Unveiled: Humanity at the Crossroads* (New York: Crossroads Publishing, 1996).

   Epigraph: Michael Cunningham, *The Hours* (New York: Picorda, 1998).

Shift 6: Embracing Difficulty

Epigraph: Pema Chödrön, "Maitri: Cultivating Unconditional Friendliness towards Oneself," from *The Love That Never Dies* workshop in Berkeley, CA (Portage, MI: Great Path, September 1997).

1. Pema Chödrön, *Start Where You Are: A Guide to Compassionate Living* (Boston: Shambhala, 2001).

2. Jacob Needleman, *Lost Christianity: A Journey of Rediscovery to the Center of the Christian Experience.*(New York: Doubleday, 1980).

3. Rumi, excerpt from "The Question," in *The Essential Rumi*, trans. Coleman Barks (San Francisco: HarperSanFrancisco, 1995).

4. Pema Chödrön, *Tonglen: The Path of Transformation* (Halifax, NS: Vajradhatu, 2001).

   Epigraph: Excerpted from *Real Happiness*. Copyright © 2010 by Sharon Salzberg. Used by permission of Workman Publishing Co., Inc., New York. All rights reserved.

5. Esther Hautzig, *The Endless Steppe: Growing Up in Siberia* (London: Thomas Y. Crowell, 1968).

6. Arlie Hochschild, *The Second Shift* (New York: Penguin, 1989).

7. "The Invitation" from *The Invitation* by ORIAH. Copyright ©1999 by Oriah Mountain Dreamer. Reprinted by permission

of HarperCollins Publishers.

Epigraph: Excerpt from "Kindness" from *Words Under the Words: Selected Poems* by Naomi Shihab Nye, copyright © 1995. Reprinted with the permission of Far Corner Books, Portland, Oregon.

8.   Ibid.

9.   Kobun Chino Otogawa Roshi, http://www.everydaydharma .org/Kobun.html.

10. Sharon Salzberg, *The Force of Kindness: Change Your Life with Compassion and Love* (Boulder, CO: Sounds True, 2010). Used by permission of Sounds True.

11. Dan Dennett, *Dan Dennett on Dangerous Memes* (TED Talk, February 2002).

Finding Balance in the Swirl

Epigraph: Ralph Waldo Emerson, *Emerson's Essay on Compensation* (Sewanee, TN: University Press of Sewanee Tennessee, 1906).

1.   Adapted excerpt from Henry David Thoreau, *Walden* (Boston, MA: Houghton, Mifflin & Co., 1854).

2.   C. S. Lewis, *Shadowlands* (1993).

ACKNOWLEDGMENTS

I'm deeply grateful to the many people who have offered support and encouragement in my journey of birthing this book. First and foremost, I offer my deepest thanks to Paul Ginter and our children, Nathan and Kenzie, for their love and support and patience and for the great blessing of living day-to-day life with such joy and magic—even in the very ordinary moments.

I feel gratitude, beyond words, to my mother, Jean Horneffer, whose support and presence I still feel daily, as well as my father, Harold Horneffer, who continues to teach me what it means to live fully and with great vitality.

I offer a heartfelt thank-you to my mother- and father-in-law, Sally and Walter Ginter. Along with their collective support, I feel honored to have learned so much about the art of writing from Sally. Her encouragement and amazing editing skills have journeyed with me for more than a decade, and this companionship has been invaluable.

A deep bow of appreciation to my editor at Hay House, Laura Koch, and my agent, Krista Goering, for believing in me and this project and for all the rich input they've offered along the way.

I'm also so grateful to my dearest friends for walking with me on this path with love, honesty, depth, and lightness. My heartfelt thanks to Patti Frawley, Diane Melvin, Mark Nepo, Susan McHenry, Heather and Jim Ratliff, Mary Anderson, Pam Poley, Pam and George deAlth, Beth Herman, Beth Luppe, Paula Chase, Catherine Ellis, Pat Huston, Gail Martin, Elena Klaw, and Lori Osborne, and, of course, my brother and sister-in-law, Mark and Beth Horneffer.

I feel similar gratitude for the companionship and support from my holistic health family: Charlene Brown, Molly Vass-Lehman, Gay Walker, Paula Jamison, Jan Dekker, Jenise Brown, Ming Chan, Michele McGrady, Tom Holmes, and Dennis Simpson.

I also want to acknowledge several teachers and guides whose words and life messages live within and through me: Patty Gatto-Waldon, Cindy Libman, Sheila Sullivan, and in loving memory of Morris Knapp, Brenda Manzano, Larry DeGoffau, and George Kitchen.

I feel humbled and thankful for the ongoing journey of listening to the larger mysteries of life and the Divine presence within them. My heartfelt thanks to all of the students, clients, and workshop participants who have given me the honor of being part of their lives and sharing in their sacred journeys of growth, awakening, and healing.

Thanks, also, to Robert Weir for his editing assistance along the way, Rachel Crabil for her assistance with acquiring permissions, and Max, for being a helpful writing companion when he wasn't attempting to eat pages from my manuscript.

ABOUT THE AUTHOR

Karen Horneffer-Ginter has been practicing psychology and teaching yoga and contemplative practices for more than 16 years. She has also taught graduate students and health-care professionals, along with directing a university-based holistic health care program and co-founding the Center for Psychotherapy and Wellness in Kalamazoo, Michigan.

The aim of Karen's work is to reconnect people with the wisdom of their inner life by reclaiming what gets lost amid the busyness of day-to-day life: qualities such as stillness, self-care, creativity, joy, humor, gratitude, and compassion. Her intention is to support people in finding a sense of balance and sacredness in their lives.

For more information, please visit her websites at www.karenhg.com and www.fullcupthirstyspirit.com.

Hay House Titles of Related Interest

YOU CAN HEAL YOUR LIFE, the movie,
starring Louise L. Hay & Friends
(available as a 1-DVD program and an expanded 2-DVD set)
Watch the trailer at: **www.LouiseHayMovie.com**

THE SHIFT, the movie,
starring Dr. Wayne W. Dyer
(available as a 1-DVD program and an expanded 2-DVD set)
Watch the trailer at: **www.DyerMovie.com**

✦◇✦

A DAILY DOSE OF SANITY: A Five-Minute Soul Recharge for Every Day of the Year, by Alan Cohen

THE MINDFUL MANIFESTO: How Doing Less and Noticing More Can Help Us Thrive in a Stressed-Out World, by Dr. Jonty Heaversedge and Ed Haliwell

SHIFT HAPPENS: How to Live an Inspired Life . . . Starting Right Now! by Robert Holden

SOUL-CENTERED: Transform Your Life in 8 Weeks with Meditation, by Sarah McLean

All of the above are available at your local bookstore,
or may be ordered by contacting Hay House (see next page).

✦◇✦

We hope you enjoyed this Hay House Insights book. If you'd like to receive our online catalog featuring additional information on Hay House books and products, or if you'd like to find out more about the Hay Foundation, please contact:

INSIGHTS

Hay House, Inc., P.O. Box 5100, Carlsbad, CA 92018-5100
(760) 431-7695 or (800) 654-5126
(760) 431-6948 (fax) or (800) 650-5115 (fax)
www.hayhouse.com® • **www.hayfoundation.org**

✦◇✦

Published and distributed in Australia by: Hay House Australia Pty. Ltd., 18/36 Ralph St., Alexandria NSW 2015 • *Phone:* 612-9669-4299 *Fax:* 612-9669-4144 • www.hayhouse.com.au

Published and distributed in the United Kingdom by:
Hay House UK, Ltd., 292B Kensal Rd., London W10 5BE • *Phone:* 44-20-8962-1230 • *Fax:* 44-20-8962-1239 • www.hayhouse.co.uk

Published and distributed in the Republic of South Africa by:
Hay House SA (Pty), Ltd., P.O. Box 990, Witkoppen 2068
Phone/Fax: 27-11-467-8904 • www.hayhouse.co.za

Published in India by: Hay House Publishers India, Muskaan Complex, Plot No. 3, B-2, Vasant Kunj, New Delhi 110 070 • *Phone:* 91-11-4176-1620 *Fax:* 91-11-4176-1630 • www.hayhouse.co.in

Distributed in Canada by: Raincoast, 9050 Shaughnessy St., Vancouver, B.C. V6P 6E5 • *Phone:* (604) 323-7100 *Fax:* (604) 323-2600 • www.raincoast.com

✦◇✦

Take Your Soul on a Vacation

Visit **www.HealYourLife.com®** to regroup, recharge, and reconnect with your own magnificence. Featuring blogs, mind-body-spirit news, and life-changing wisdom from Louise Hay and friends.

Visit **www.HealYourLife.com**

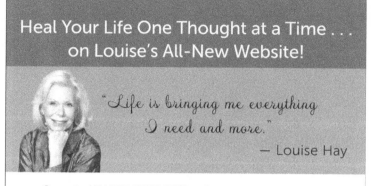